AF447941

Climbing Life's Mountain

Climbing Life's Mountain

Ramona Seath Lübke

Ramona Publishing

Copyright © 2024 by Ramona Seath Lübke

All rights reserved. No part of this book may be reproduced in any manner whatsoever without written permission except in the case of brief quotations embodied in critical articles and reviews.

First Printing, 2024

OUR FATHER WHICH ART IN
HEAVEN, HALLOWED BE THY NAME.
THY KINGDOM COME.
THY WILL BE DONE IN EARTH,
AS IT IS IN HEAVEN.
GIVE US THIS DAY OUR DAILY BREAD.
AND FORGIVE US OUR DEBTS,
AS WE FORGIVE OUR DEBTORS.
AND LEAD US NOT INTO TEMPTATION,
BUT DELIVER US FROM EVIL:
FOR THINE IS THE KINGDOM, AND THE
POWER,
AND THE GLORY FOREVER...AMEN

Matthew 6:9-13

Contents

Memories

Evart native wins Angel Award

by David Moe, Editor

EVART — Take popular gospel singer Sandy Patty's voice, smooth off the rough edges, and you can easily understand why Ramona Seath-Lubke was the winner in the music category for the 18th Annual Angel Awards this past February in Hollywood.

The International Angel Awards stand for excellence in moral, spiritual and social impact in all forms of media — motion picture, television, books, albums, stage, video and radio.

Billed only under her first name, "Ramona," she won her angel award for her album, "Serenity."

"My producer, John Grover Lewis first worked with me to get it right. I couldn't believe it when I was nominated, and when (my album) won, I knew it was God working through John."

"I suppose what has made Ramona an inspiration to many is her ability to live a simple, Christ-centered life while maintaining a growing understanding of God's most spectacular universe," Lewis said. "This kind of inspiration is heard throughout her music. What resolve it must take to sing highly majestic *words of God with honest simplicity ...* Therein rests the extraordinary power of Ramona's gifts."

Although she holds a music minor, Ramona is a registered nurse and holds a degree in psychology from St. Joseph's College in Windham, Maine. Shortly after college, however, she surrendered her career in medicine for marriage and a family.

Although raised in a Christian home, it was only after some tragic life experiences that Ramona finally gave her talent to the Lord. The first came when she witnessed every parent's horror — the death of her 2-1/2 year-old son by being crushed to death between

Ramona with producer John Grover Lew[is] following presentation.

two automobiles — the second when her happy hom[e] ended in divorce. A third came when the doctors d[is]covered that this mother of five (four surviving) h[ad] a growth in her throat.

"The surgery devastated my singing voic[e,]" Ramona says. "When I'd put my little boy to bed, h[e'd] ask me why my voice sounded so funny. Then [I'd] smile at him and kiss him good night, and go off [to] cry alone." She says it took years of work for her vo[ice] to return.

Although she has had substantial voice training a[nd] has been in concert in Michigan, California, Ma[ine,] Hawaii and England, for many years she sang o[nly]

continued, pag[e]

MISSION LANDS

Siblings

Brothers Edward, Jack, and Robert (my twin)

Brother Edward

Sister Maxine

Maternal
Great-grandfather

Maternal
Grandparents

Father

Mother

Children

Mark

Mona (Ramona)

Mark's Grave

Debra

William and Louis

Children & Grandchildren

SEVENTH DAY ADVENTIST CHURCH
SABBATH SERVICES
9:15-12:00
SECRET PLACE   OCT 3
SPEAKER MARI HASHIKAWA
CONCERT BY
RAMONA SEATH-LUBKE

Chapter 1

Back In Time

BORN THIS DAY ... March 24, 1929...In the village of Evart, Michigan. As I grew into a child of more understanding, little did I know how many winding roads were before me as I began life's journey to "life's mountaintop"...

Living at my grandparent's farm with my mother just before I left Michigan for nurse's training in Tennessee.

I early learned that my father was taken from us children. My twin and I were 18 months of age when he passed, leaving my mother to care for us twins, two other sons and a daughter. I love to joggle my memory to bring forth all the wonderful memories life has given me...and of course in doing so one must be exposed to times of mistakes and horrible heartaches. I like to take that risk, for it gives me opportunity to make things right with others and with God. I especially like how much it helps me grow into a wiser and more kind, loving woman. Have you ever thought upon the darkness that would surround us if we never took inventory of our lives...just how much others would suffer along with our careless attitude? Oh, how we always need to be aware of how our thoughts, words and actions affect the world around us each day of our lives.

As I think about writing to mankind I especially want my readers to know that no matter how beautiful my life may seem to you, there are always untold stories that weren't so lovely...meaning all of us have done some things that make us wish we could start life over again, and...you know the reason we don't always reveal everything, is to protect the innocent! There are so many moments that I still feel the agony of how my decisions destroyed the happiness and contentment of others...especially my children when divorce knocked at our door. Oh, how I wish I could go back and seek other ways to find solutions. I know there are times that divorce is the only way, but I urge folk before taking those steps to think through how divorce can be avoided, that innocent children are not left in a dark valley. If we have God in our life all things can lead to a more satisfactory outcome, not only for the innocent, but for us. God was so good to have given me beautiful, well-adjusted children in spite of my weaknesses at their vulnerable age.

My first very sad memory is remembering sitting snuggled by my momma on the sofa while she did some mending...it was Sunday...small tears trickled down her cheeks. When age of better understanding complimented my wisdom I was told that *SUNDAYS* were difficult for my loving mother...that was the day daddy used to take her for a ride in the country.

Because I had a well-structured, loving Christian mother, there were many sweet memories of a fatherless home. Yet the vacancy of a loving father tore at my heart many times over. Yes, there are homes with fathers that perhaps are cruel and missing in action, but never does a child do away with the longing for the loving connection of a father. School functions found me many times sitting off by myself on a lonely bench...I watched all the other children receiving attention from a daddy and oh, how I wanted to be one of them. This is how my "climbing the mountain" started!

We were privileged back then to spend much time outdoors...walking, which our mom did with us every Sabbath afternoon...after church and a light lunch. During the week we were permitted to play outdoors after school until dark. However, we first had to do our studies and practice the piano. We had grandparents in the country...7 miles out of town. Many times we would walk there or grandpa would take us home with him when he and grandmother were in town shopping. There is so much learning and joy spending time with grandparents. I thank Jesus everyday of my life for all the times I was privileged to be with them. My most endearing memories there include times of learning to ride grandpa's horse...Major...I can still hear grandma saying: "Sid, that girl is going to fall off that horse," but grandpa said: "Martha she will be ok."

Well, the inevitable happened...just around 5 years of age I had my first horrible fall while speeding around the back yard. Yes, of course grandma kept her silence...she knew grandpa felt bad enough. Sweet memories of playing with my dolls and doll buggy near the apple orchard still touch my heart today as I pass by the old homestead. That orchard still remains today, but with much less apples...the pear tree is still bringing forth fruit.

I loved all the trees and my favorite tree had a swing made from a rubber tire...later changed to a board. As I matured, a neighbor girl found her way into my heart. She lived a few farms away and had several beautiful horses...bareback and long blond hair a flowing found us riding over the hills and in the valley's until we could hardly walk after dismounting :). I still love to think of all the times she and I would lay in bed at night, when I was privileged to stay overnight, and talk about things that cheered us, but sometimes wondered in thought to what things were going to be like when we grew up and maybe moved away or such. Yes, we did separate when I left for Washington. I must confess, I played with my dolls and buggy until about 12 years old. WHAT??? teenagers would say today! A long childhood is something that never should be taken from us...

Since there were five of us children, mother divided duties between us...set the table, clear the table, wash the dishes, wipe the dishes and sweep the kitchen floor. It was wonderful that we only had to dust once in 5 weeks. I would tell my mom I was "allergic" to dust, but she would respond always..."that's OK dearie, just keep dusting." The boys got to vacuum. I called my mother *mummy* much of the time...when I was on good terms. Mother had very long curls...very very pretty brown hair as I remember...I was told daddy had very curly hair.

It seems since we didn't have a daddy the uncles were always wanting to *spoil* us. I can remember so clearly as a very young child sitting on the back porch waiting for the sun to go down on Sabbath evening so my uncle Bob could take us downtown for an *ice cream cone*. Mom would always make certain we didn't break the edges of the Holy Sabbath Day.

I loved Friday nights...Mother would act out our Sabbath School lesson by using Anagrams to build cities and forts!

It was such a privilege to get to ride to a bigger town or city...going to Grand Rapids, Flint and Detroit Michigan were the highlights of childhood.

I grew up with a sister that was 10 years older and a brother that was 8 years older...so you see, I had plenty of discipline. It wasn't all bad, however. My sis would make us the best peanut brittle and chocolate fudge and my brother would bring us little goodies from the small-town gas station where he was employed. The younger boys helped till the ground and plant veggies at my grandparents' farm. My brother Jack was 4 years older, and didn't care to be among our disciplinarians, but kept us entertained by his wonderful sense of humor, which always had some interesting story attached to it! Of course, my twin, though 15 minutes younger, took it upon himself to help me grow up to be a young woman of sensibility, charming and with a soft kind heart. Around the age of 10 he would always say: "men do not like bold girls" if I did something that was out of line...so he thought.

A few years after daddy was accidentally killed my mom started working at the Evart telephone office. I loved visiting her there. To this day I still love to think about plugging in those plugs and pulling that little switch...it was amazing how it worked. Sometimes, though, my big sis and brother were watching over me while mom was at work during the night hours, I would awaken and feel lonesome or a little scared so I would call her. She suggested that I walk to her place of work, which was a couple blocks from our house. I responded quickly that I was too scared to walk there alone because someone might grab me. She sweetly said: "when they come to a streetlight, they will let you go"...but I said: 'what if they don't come to a street light?' Today, a parent would never suggest such activity for a young child. Those sweet days are gone forever, are they not?

My uncles got us little red wagons and tricycles...what a joy they were. Many children were not so privileged. We were just coming out of the depression!

I loved the folk that we became close to at church...what a joy they were. The Servoces, Hicks, Grace Bentley, Kittrells, and others of whom I can't remember their names. About the age of 9 or 10 our whole Sabbath School class of children learned all the memory verses for the quarter (13 Sabbaths). It was even put in the "Our Little Friend"...the church Sabbath School magazine for children.

We had many winters of sledding, throwing snowballs and at the grandparents' farm. Those were such awesome times...the snow and wind whirling and blowing...even singing through the cracks and around the windows. I loved those sounds and how cozy it was to cuddle up in the down blankets that grandmammy made with my feet on a warmed-up cast iron small skillet or such.

Perhaps one of my fondest memories was when all of us cousins got together in the summertime at the grandparents. Cousins, aunties and uncles came from all around creating lasting beautiful memories that to this day bring so much comfort. At this time in my journey...only just a few cousins remain...One time we all gathered outside the farmhouse to have a talent show. Each cousin did their "thing" ...I only remember that I chose to sing "Over the Rainbow" and though my twin seldom praised me, this day he said loudly: "that was beautiful". Around the age of 10 I took that as a good sign to make singing one of my careers.

In the year of 1941, I had an uncle that came to Michigan to visit his parents...my grandparents. He had moved to the state of Washington. Though my grandparents begged him not to leave home, he couldn't resist the urge to "go west." When he and his wife (both still quite young) decided it was time to return home they began earnestly begging my mother to take me home with them. To Washington I went. Being first acquainted with the giant hills (mountains) - to this day brings breathtaking moments that leaves a longing for the "west" that shall never depart from my soul! Those were wonderful times, but of course longing for my mother crept in strongly at times. I guess the fact that my aunt made me clothing for every activity soothed my little spirit to get me through those sad times. They provided me with a lovely horse, ice skates...even let me help pound in nails to the siding of a new house they were building. The greatest joy was climbing part of Mount Rainier.

I have so many to thank for all the beauty and wisdom graced to my life. Because of all that has gone on before me in my stepping path I am who I am today. What an awesome Heavenly Father to give me SO much at such an early age in life. I am especially grateful for all the love from blood relatives...for my dear sweet cousin Mary Elizabeth. She still walks this earth *and* lives not too far away from my dwellings. She makes the best veggie soup AND is my only close playmate still upon this earth! I do have one more special cousin (playmate), but unfortunately, he lives many towns away from me. At 94, it is such a joy to me to live close to loved ones near my age.

After I spent a few months in the state of Washington, the Japanese bombed Pearl Harbor on December 7, 1941. The United States declared war on Japan, and World War II began. Within 3 days, after Germany and Italy declared war also...the United States became fully engaged. That is when the strong love of a mother got on the phone and asked for my return home. I was put on a bus to travel back to Michigan...feeling very sad and suddenly disrupted. All the happenings around me gave me somewhat of a little "fright"...my young Japanese school mates were abruptly taken out of school and sent to who knows where...it was all very heart breaking. And not only that heartache, but at the early age of twelve I had to be subject to a very heartbroken aunt and uncle. Perhaps silently they had hoped that my mom would let me stay with them.

I got to stay with my mom for a while, but it wasn't any time at all until I was summoned to go live with my sister in Flint, Michigan. Her husband joined the Air Force (Air Corps at that time) and I was to help out with the children. Though my sis was kind, no one bends a little at times like a mother! Sometimes my tears would become many, but all in all it turned out to be one of the most wonderful experiences of my young adult life. I got to attend a Christian academy, and it was there where God became very personal in my life. The Evangelists in town at the time (the Venden brothers) were instrumental in helping me learn an everlasting love for God. They spent much time with me...picked me up for meetings and took me under their wings many times during my early teens. Though all these wonderful folk are no longer upon this earth, their wonderful Christian guidance still speaks to me today. My twin, Robert James, also was able to join me at my sisters to attend the rest of our time at Flint Jr. Academy. Being separated from a twin is like swimming against a one-way current that sees no tomorrow. Twin attachment is irreplaceable...and it forms a lifelong bond that nothing can take from us. Saying "goodbye" to him when he no longer could hold on upon this earth...my heart gave way to a lifeless existence momentarily. However, I knew he would want me to be a strength to all mankind that would encourage others to keep walking safely and happily, so with that thought I keep the faith and courage to continue on. He and I loved all the times of getting together...sometimes we would meet at a shopping mall to shop together and have lunch. He loved buying me clothes. The most endearing times were when I visited the small church where he preached many a Sabbath. I would sing and play the piano and he would bless the congregation with his touching sermons. I then got to spend a few days with him at his home near Flint, Michigan. Those were some of the most precious days of my life. I learned so much from his way of life and all the wisdom he seemed to accumulate through his earthly walk and military life. All my brothers did time in the military. My brother Edward was in the Marines and endured the battle of Guadalcanal and battle of Tarawa...he was very blessed to come back home, as he endured some very challenging times in both battles.

After church today the country of my youth seemed to be calling me...the skies were decorated with clouds of spectacular formation. How sweet it was to watch the beauty of corn fields go passing by, while trees were making arches over my head. Isn't it wonderful how God's creation comes to us in so many forms and in breathtaking ways? I have been alive long enough to have been taken through many striking moments of extreme weather conditions, blue skies, cloudy skies, awe-inspiring skies, magnificent mountain climbs (only one I made to the top)...Smile! I will never forget the thrill at viewing my first mountain...to this day my whole being tingles each time mountains come into view! Yes, I even experienced the shaking of earth and movement of flying objects during California earthquakes...and even one in Alaska!

There were so many folks that made lasting imprints upon my being during my stay with my sister...folk who were aware that I had a life without a father and was separated from my mother. They were so gentle and caring! Oh, how much my life was influenced by those years of separation from my mother. However, I will always be grateful to my sister for her teaching and caring for me during my important years of growth. Also, her husband (Ronald Straw) gave much of his time for me when he returned from the Air Corps. Because of him I still am playing tennis today. He made certain I learned it well...I am not a pro but can still send a pretty good serve at 95. I encourage all of you to look back upon your life journey and give thanks to all that made a difference in your life.

I would like to pause for a moment here to share this past week with my son William. He took me to a cabin on the lake in the town where the Lübke grandparents lived. This happened to be the "Blue Moon" time. With a beautiful fire pit a-glowing and quietly watching the sky across the lake, all of a sudden, our eyes captured the rising of this beautiful *blue moon*...what a never to be forgotten moment in time. It cast its brilliance upon the moving waters...*telling me, all is well with my soul!* Oh, what an awesome God we have in the heavens.

The days of Mother and Son together never go without precious memories to carry us sweetly through our journey to the end.

Our week also had stargazing, wilderness hikes and sand dunes to walk. A walk to the lighthouse along Lake Michigan shore will be one of the most glorious events of my entire life! At 95, what a blessing to be blessed with mobility and yes, even tennis playing at the high school. My son has now returned to his home across the miles, but he always leaves me with another together date to bring comfort and joy.

Chapter 2

College Days

How quickly life moves on...Flint Jr. Academy had only 11 grades so I had to look for a school to complete my last year of high school. Oh how sad it was to hug my school mates for the last time, as all of us ended up in different schools. For a short time I went to Adelphian Academy in Holly, Michigan. I loved it there but found it too fatiguing...it was several miles away and the drive took too much precious time away from study and home. I remember the teachers and folk there, so kind and regretful that I had to leave. I found a lovely school near to where my sister lived and happily enjoyed every moment there. It was not a Christian school like I had been so used to, but it did open my eyes to many new ways of lifestyle. Though the students and teachers lived a much different way of life than I had been raised with, I was treated with great respect and included in all the fun activities. In fact, I was voted the prettiest senior of the year---(I mention this because the class was trying hard to make me feel wanted in spite of coming in the last minute to graduate) and they also asked me to sing "The Holy City" for Baccalaureate service. Their kindness never fades away. Things seemed so much different back then. My heart aches at times to watch how some youth are treated today by their own.

Soon after graduation I was taken up north to be with my mother...it was with her that I was to work at Reed City Hospital. Since mother had been working there for some time and won the hearts of doctors and nursing staff, I was somewhat privileged early to kindness and respect. I am to this day still awed by the tall, beautiful impressionable Director of Nurses. I had never nor since been so charmed with someone of her position nor strength of character. I also shall never forget the first night of *nurses aide* duty...driving home from night shift I still can remember how I fought to stay awake. I never did well at night shift!!! In fact when I entered nurses training the staff tried to prevent me as much as possible from "night duty."

This was a very teachable time for me...not only by my mother, but the doctors and other nurses took me under their wings. I am so happy to say that the Director of Nurses (her name just came to me...surprising me greatly...Ms. Raarup) also gave me special attention. I so wish she was alive today so I could let her know just how much joy and growth she brought to my life. She even let me listen to the radio at work when Princess Elizabeth got married in November of 1947. As I write many sweet memories are surfacing, which gives me a bit of sadness...sadness that I failed to make known to many of the folk how some of their caring, wonderful teachings and way of life affected me so beautifully today. It is my prayer that those reading my words upon these pages will be inspired to reach out to those that helped them along the way, while they still walk the earth with them. There are so many without loved ones and significant others that continue to do good for others in spite of their unhappy circumstances. It is with a tender heart that we can help lift up folk from all walks of life. Many appear that "all is ok," but if we start looking beyond we will discover many bleeding hearts. Though we know the world is heading down a dark path--------let us work on keeping a joyful heart and trust that God will always be with us. Remember, God said: "Whosever believeth in Him will have everlasting life." Though we seem to be forced to accept the reality of today, rather than true reality, we still must stand strong in our knowledge of truth.

The year with my mom before departing for nurses training went by rapidly. As I look back now, it brings tears to my eyes...I never again had that privilege again of being side-by-side day after day. Why is it these loving moments strike us so tenderly? Being a young woman and apparently attractive to men brought some scary times...meaning, I no longer had the protection of my brothers, they had gone their ways to serve our country at that time. Being somewhat naive because of that protection took me some places that, had it not been for God's watch care over me, I would have disheartening stories to tell. I learned quickly how being protected does not always end up in our favor...

I did date a young pilot, but that relationship only led to sadness. He fell deeply in love with me, but I did care for him very much. The fact that I had early on in life made up my mind I wanted to become a nurse gave me courage not to lose sight of my goal. Also I had made up my mind that I wanted to marry a minister. Though in my early college days I did date a ministerial student, that also turned out to be very disappointing. No matter how much I tried to keep in mind my marriage preference it seemed I always ended up dating out of my liking. It seemed doctors. lawyers, professors and musicians followed my trail more readily because there were few ministers around at the time of my dating! I want to be honest. I did have married men of different professions try pursuing me. When young we just aren't equipped to say "no" in a kind loving way. I am so thankful that God seemed to always be there and because of a Christian upbringing I did have tools that saved me many times from dreadful consequences.

I would like to take another pause here. When revealing all that goes into climbing life's mountain there are moments worthy of attention. I am certain there will be several pauses as I keep climbing! Today was a tender day and one of gratefulness...I early met someone at my car in the parking lot to pick up a vacuum...it turned out that she put the vacuum back in her car and said: "let me go with you." It is so unbelievable at times how God is so merciful in spite of our carelessness. I love Lamentations 3: 22-23. "It is the LORD'S mercies that we are not consumed because his compassions fail not. They are new every morning: great is thy faithfulness."

As I dusted and cleaned all the sinks and bathtubs, memories of my mom and all the times I lived there after her final departure rushed in melting my heart! I am SO thankful for all those precious memories, because it means God has blessed me with many wonderful times of treasured happenings. Oh, how touching now to look back. With tender tears I sail away to yesterdays!

It was time to seek a college, but the thought of leaving my mom and place of birth seemed to hit me with sudden fear--fear of leaving stable, familiar surroundings and those that loved and cared for me. It kept going through my mind just what it would be like to be thrown into a completely new atmosphere. Somehow, with the encouragement of family and friends I did respond yes to my acceptance at Madison College Tennessee. This college was suggested because my sister's father-in-law was President there (W.E. Straw). He had been the dean of EMC (which now is Andrews University in Berrien Springs, Michigan) and I had the privilege of spending time with he and his wife when I was a 13 year old. I must say I learned very much about eating a healthy diet and also about my sweet Lord in their household.

Mrs. Straw was the *angel type* where Mr. Straw was, let's say a little on the conservative side. However, he did have this wonderful charming sense of humor...therefore these facts sent me on my way to Madison College. I stayed there 3 weeks. Then, one day when no one was watching too closely I boarded a bus back to Michigan. Today I cannot imagine me doing such a thing. It is amazing how loneliness and the unknown can drive us to bravery such as I pursued! I was SO happy to be home, but sorry to say it did not last long. Soon thereafter my brother-in-law (President Straw's son) put me back on the bus saying: "Even though you are confused and heartbroken just now, one day you will be thankful I did this." With brokenness and tears streaming, my family had to watch and hold back their tears for being seemingly the "guilty party."

Soon, college life seemed to fit me well. There were some trials in my early start that could have driven me home again, but somehow courage and strength from above carried me through to victory over the hurt that sometimes can come about from disturbed minds. Meaning, others can be drawn into thinking things that are not an issue due to their own insecurity. As I look back, I wonder how I ever came through with an understanding heart that drew some of us together in spite of some not so good experiences.

I was asked to do speeches for some of the Friday evening functions and also had the privilege of being in some of the short plays.

I went to college with a background in some piano training and a vocal talent. Since my sister's sister-in-law was married to the Professor of Music I was encouraged to minor in music. Nursing was my major, of course, which gave me little time for practice. Professor Mitzelfelt seemed to just ignore the heavy schedule placed upon nursing students and signed me up for piano, flute, violin and vocal training. I was pushed so hard that soon I was playing flute in band and violin in the orchestra. I was not that accomplished at all...just made to believe it had to be done and there was no other choice. How I managed to pass everything is certainly one of those miracles that pop out of nowhere. I am thankful today for all that took place at college, but still wonder how I ever got through without failing a course or two. I also worked on the farm the first year...maybe that was what gave me peace through all the turmoil. I believe every person, male and female should have a time of *working on a farm.* It teaches us so many things about animals and God's creation. Every worker, teacher, pastor and student contributed to part of who I am today. I think about how sweet all of them were to me. I especially remember the joyous attitude of the laundry manager...he always had a wonderful way of creating laughter, yet had moments where he expressed his sweet love for Jesus. My most unforgettable experience in my junior year of nursing was when the chief of surgery asked me to remove an appendix. I had scrubbed in several times with this doctor and thought he would never ask this of a nurse...only the resident doctor. He was very picky and sort of arrogant, but an excellent surgeon. I did it and the patient did well. I think the doctor wanted to find out just how well I had been paying attention to details. I did find out later that the professor liked my progress in schooling, and even my chemistry professor was trying to get me to enter medical school. I probably should have gone to medical school for I not only had concern for the well being of my patients, but cared deeply about the skills of the physician. Some of the residents would call me out at night to start blood transfusions. I thought that a little bit unusual back in my day...hmmm.

Early in my nursing adventure I was dating a resident. This did not set too well with my superior student nurses. Because I did my best to make them feel loved and special all turned out well. He joined the Navy and soon departed for overseas. We really cared for each other, but someone else took advantage of his absence and sad to say...hearts were broken.

All too soon it was time to close college doors and move on to my next adventure. I shall always be grateful for the love, caring and wonderful teachings at Madison College...so much that I learned there has kept me focused on a magnificent kind loving Heavenly Father. Each day I feel more and more close to God...and pray that that glorious feeling will overflow to those that long for a sweeter walk with Jesus.

> *Blessed are they which do hunger*
> *and thirst after righteousness:*
> *for they shall be filled...*
>
> *Matthew 5:6*

Chapter 3

Lincoln Nebraska/Loma Linda California

Shortly after I graduated from nurses training at Madison College, I married a man I met there. Our wedding was one never to be forgotten...my soon-to-be father-in-law was the professor of music at the college. Since he was lord over the orchestra, that is what we were privileged to have for a huge beautiful wedding. And to top it off my husband's grandfather married us...He was the president of Madison College...father of my husband's mother.

My new husband had been accepted into the premed course at Union College, so soon were on our way to a new destination. The autumn leaves were making their way to the ground and the days were becoming a little bit more chilly as we snuggled into our apartment at Union College, Lincoln, Nebraska. I always loved the Autumns...as a child in Michigan

I always was so deeply touched by the magnificent change of colors...from green to orange, gold, red and amber. My mother and grandmother loved to bake pumpkin and apple pies at this time of year. I can still smell the tantalizing aroma from the kitchen. We didn't get a lot of goodies, because both parent and grandparents kept us on a watchful path of healthy living.

After all the splendor of our wedding, there were some beautiful moments at Lincoln. While there, I gave birth to a charming baby girl. my nephew came to live with us for one school year...he was 13...very wise and brilliant and found it difficult to study because of it. However, he finally finished the 8th grade and returned home to Michigan to later in life become a highly respected Michigan State Policeman...meaning doing other duties of which is not for me to disclose. My husband directed the college choir, which was so beautiful. I want to thank all the folk at Union College for making my stay there very sweet.

After my husband finished premed, we departed Union College for Loma Linda University where he had been accepted into Medical School. Life had been so beautiful for a time, but it is a cruel world that, at times, places us in positions where we never intended to be. It was at Loma Linda where my husband and I parted ways, and our marriage became a statistic. After our parting, he became not only a physician, but traveled the world directing famous choirs. He was even was invited to the most prestigious Carnegie Hall. Though our life together ended abruptly we always kept that respect for each other. I was told by his wife, who still keeps in touch with me that "you were the love of his life." He is no longer upon this earth but as I had said before...all of us need to take ownership to failures in a marriage. Let's be honest, each of us have many things that we mourn in this life. There are many things to be thankful for in this marriage...I had excellent music training in voice, piano, flute and violin...or should I say I didn't have much of a choice. Any family member was expected by the father to devote a considerable amount of time and energy to prepare for placement in band and orchestra or both! Today, others can reap all that Maestro Harold Mitzelfelt taught me along with my grandmother and mother.

I filed for divorce in Las Vegas...an experience that certainly gave me a quick education. I was subjected to a sudden change of voyage in my life...there were many folk there that made my stay very intriguing, yet also left me feeling a little nervous at times due to all the glamour, lights and actors. I suppose telling a few experiences will cause somewhat of a problem...meaning my readers might find it difficult to picture how this young unknown had all these wonderful moments. I found myself sitting alone one evening waiting for a show to happen when a young Elvis asked if he could sit at my table. He was just starting out and perhaps he thought I might be a young starlet with aspirations just like him. It was so many years ago I only remember that we had a Coca Cola and then parted ways. I'm sure he was just as uncomfortable as I, but I do remember he was very sweet and also extremely good looking! Then there was a time that I was getting ready to swim at the fancy hotel where I was staying...all of a sudden I hear a voice being directed my way and along side that voice that called me I noticed Liberace. They both were in the pool and offered me a rum and coke. I took it, but fortunately I only took a sip or two...my first alcohol beverage ever, and I must say, there were no further problems with alcoholic drinking! It was awesome that they did get out of the pool and let me look inside Liberace's car...the upholstery was designed in the shape of a keyboard. There were some other people of interest, but with less excitement.

Though I was much relieved at the end of my time in Vegas I want to say I was very benefited by all the attractions and attention given to me while in this setting. Shortly before I announced my soon departure I was asked by two different hotels if I would care to stay and be a dancer. Since I had not been auditioned as yet, I presumed maybe they were just looking at "legs". However, I had studied some ballet and perhaps it came up in one of our conversations. I am very thankful that my ego didn't take over...that my upbringing spoke loud and clear. What seems a wonderful happening at the time can later become a very heartbreaking experience down the road. Many times in my life I have thanked the Lord for the Holy Spirit that saved me from disasters. In fact when we get to heaven we will learn all the times we were saved from death and ugly outcomes had we not been guided by the Almighty One. I am reminded of Psalm 32:7 - You are a hiding place for me; you preserve me from trouble; you surround me with shouts of deliverance.

At this point in time I am thinking about how I live my life...and what I am doing to help folk of today and the next generations. Divorce was not an option in our household. I begin to feel the results of a broken home...our little girl and all the repercussions of sudden change. My family was far from happy with my decision of divorce and let me know by saying hurtful words. They even shunned me for a time. I chose to take the quiet approach...not wanting to make me look better at the expense of my husband's unhappiness. It was kind of my older brother to come to my rescue with words to my family: "in spite of what you feel inside and what I don't know; you can rest assured that Ramona had a very good reason for doing what she did."

Since many love the chronicling of my journey I find it very difficult at times to bring forward all that should be said at the best times...meaning, I want so much to share all that had specific effect upon my life journey that can help others that pass through similar circumstances. Also, it is my desire to make known to those that helped me develop a beautiful story of my life. Of course when one lives the length of time that I have, many cannot be "thanked", but maybe their loved ones and friends can reap the rewards.

Being young, and alone, I felt as a tiny speck. Although I do believe all of us are or can be a mighty waterfall...giving drinks to the thirsty and watering one another's garden. Though in a little corner I wanted to see the hands reaching out to me...just stop and say to someone, "I love you"...unlock the good within me and leave a flower behind.

I had become so disheartened that the blinds stayed down...now they climbed high...the trees were greener, the mountains magnificent and the ocean became my frequent walk. As a very young child my parents and grandparents introduced me to a beautiful world...I loved nature...the out-doors, walking...and all the beauty in the day and night sky...I especially remember when in the country going to the porch during the night many times...just to stare at the sky. Only if you have done this or do this do you understand what one feels during times such as this.

Seasons came and seasons went but I seemed to scale new heights...mental monuments did I create, but yet to know it was the light that chases away the darkness. I needed to fully surrender ALL TO JESUS!

My nursing degree came in very handy now that I was caring for myself. Because of this my daughter was placed in her father's care...I feel it best not to enlarge on this that feelings are not trampled upon. During a lifetime we find many things that have been taken away that bring many a tear and pain. Oh, how much we have to learn through sorrows. All the folk that were part of that time left me with everlasting, kind loving imprints. Many of the doctors and nurses also gave their sweet time and energy toward my healing and recovery.

At this moment I am praying that each word or experience my memory has brought forth and will bring forth, that it somehow will find a place in your life to give you peace in solving some of your troubles and provide ways to better yourself. We must remember at all times that each day we are giving and receiving. Every single day is an opportunity to learn and grow...AND to let things of importance flow freely to a world of possibilities. Our first priority is to have a prayer and read something from God's word...in doing this we are equipped with knowledge and understanding to help others find their way more easily. Whatever we are given should be to share with our loved ones and our fellowman.

Chapter 4

The Sweet and The Broken

Many steps up the mountain, but much much more to climb. Today as I was thinking about what I should make known to you next, I wandered off into my music room. My life from a young child calls me often into my world of music. It is there I get lost in the classics, like Beethoven, Brahms, Mozart and Rachmaninoff especially carry me off into dreamland...meaning the depth and beauty pull me into a place where I see or feel nothing but the most powerful and beautiful sensation of all that can be felt as a human being...I love how some of these composers challenged the rules. Yes, the past romance's are forever in my soul and never lose the *power* to bring back all that the body and mind can feel beyond all perception. Nothing ugly appears...only the beautiful...like the touch of a hand, or the vision of love from one that radiates a deep powerful mental image that leaves one enchanted for hours...it's such a beautiful and peaceful place to be...

One day while at work at a Riverside hospital in California where I was employed as Head Nurse on the Medical unit, one of my nurse friends asked me to go with her to the mountains because two of the *interns* from a near-by hospital had asked her to join them and to bring a friend there on a certain night. Long story short...my friend became ill but insisted on my going without her, for the "young doctors would be disappointed if neither of us showed up." I was told which intern I was to be connected with, however, he seemed to be enjoying his "drinks" a little too much so the other intern took it upon himself to step in and make it known to his friend that he was going to take me home. I was so comforted with the change of plans. Of course my partner for the night was not at all pleased with the outcome. I am so happy to say that eventually things settled down and a romance came out of that night of frustrations. In fact, we were so delighted to find out that we both came from towns in Michigan that were only short miles apart.

We had many sweet dates but soon the internship was over...I returned to Michigan and my boyfriend had to leave for the service. I learned so many wonderful lessons from this love experience in California and want also to thank everyone who shared this beautiful time with me.

I was feeling the sadness that follows sudden separation, and wondered when would we see each other again. In that moment of loneliness I hear the sound of ringing...I picked up the phone and to my surprise it was the voice of my doctor friend asking me to come to Texas. He wanted to marry me but he didn't propose until after I got off the plane. He bought me a lovely light blue dress and invited some of his Army friends to join us for our wedding. It was as sweet and beautiful as any wedding could be. When two people are so much in love and God is joining them in Holy Matrimony...how could anything be more glorious than that?

Permit me to step aside briefly to tell you where I am...it is December 24, 2023, near Boston Massachusetts...where along with my son William, his wife, his in-laws and my daughter are about to depart for Christmas Eve Mass. I am not of that faith, however, they always have wonderful Christmas Eve programs and it brings us sweetly to the feel of Christ and His wonderful birth. The service was lovely and as we departed the fresh rain had left its smell of freshness to a fairly comfortable evening as we walked to our cars and drove back to the in-laws for a wonderful Christmas Eve dinner.

The next morning we were joyed by gift opening with all the loved ones and even got to take a long walk in the sunshine. After a wonderful sweet visit Christmas dinner was tenderly shared as we made our last comments before having to say good bye for this year...the moon was shining brightly as we walked slowly to our cars...always wonder-ing if there will be a next year as this. Life has been so beautiful and so rewarding...even with the sad times included.

Arriving at my son's home after an hour's drive back to Boston found us all in a quiet mood...we seemed to feel the need to reorganize...but in a kind loving way. Soon it was time to say good night and fall asleep with tender thoughts of the last two days of family togetherness. With all that is going on in the world at this time in our lives I can't help but thank my Heavenly Father for the gifts of peace when falling asleep. My heart is always so full of sadness knowing that many folk around the world do not know the peace that we have, at least for the moment. Things could change in the twinkling of an eye!

Awakening to a beautiful morning that took us to the wonderful outdoors...my son took us to a place where tennis was available and a huge park of miles of walking was gloriously spread out all around us. The train whistle brought sounds of childhood while the soft gentle breezes passed by each footstep made in our path of glory. Night time came too quickly, for the morning was to be my last day with my son and daughter...they were always so sweet...tucking me in like a child. I guess reaching 94 + is a time to hold dear the times with a parent. And.......after all...a day of tennis and a few miles of walking is un-believable, even to me.

It is 2024 now...returning to home is always sweet, but yet a bit of loneliness brings us back to reality. The worst part of leaving children and the joy of being together gives us that wonder of...when will we have this privilege again. I am not so young anymore and each child has their duties to perform. Though that be the circumstances I am very grateful for all the times they sacrifice to be with their mother.

It is time again to continue climbing...My new husband was sent to Eniwetok Atoll in the Marshall Islands...where nuclear tests were conducted from 1948 to 1958. Perhaps the reason behind sending soldiers there after the test were completed was probably due to a strategic location for the United States in the event of any further war and of course a doctor was needed. I always thought how interesting this assignment was...*not one female was stationed there AND not even a female dog!* I have many folk during this time that I am so thankful for...all the love and support from family and even new people that came forth to encourage my new journey. We survived the separation and the years following brought us four lovely children...Debra, William, Mark and Louis.

Our first assignment after Eniwetok Atoll was Arizona, then off to Michigan for an OBGYN residency...next stop was California. Our new home took us up to the hills of Pomona California...it was so beautiful. We were surrounded by several lovely mountains and my husband loved planting roses and other colorful flowers...the hill in our huge driveway was covered with Ivy. We had so many wonderful times as a family unit...the children loved it there...enjoying all the children on the hill and all their school pals. Every Friday night my husband had the children listen to classical music. It paid off, for they made music a special part of their world. One of the most enjoyable happenings in our marriage was going to the Los Angeles symphony once every month. Those were our very happy times. We loved classical music and the tender feelings created by the beautiful music surrounding us.

It was a lovely Sunday...we got a call from a neurosurgeon colleague of my husband and his wife asking us to join them for a Sunday afternoon of friendship to be followed by an early evening meal. What I am about to say has been published in my other books: "Take My Hand Walk With Me" and "F Sharp #". Every time I find it necessary to tell this story my energy and sparkle slips quickly from me. Though it brings a horrible heartache I feel it is good for my reader to know that we can overcome the nightmares that follow such an experience. We had such a wonderful time enjoying stories and our children to be followed by a special meal. When it was time to depart for home our friends wanted to join us to look at a unique home up in the hills where we lived. They wanted our little boy to ride with them (so many folk loved our little Mark-he was a magnet...meaning he had powerful attraction). Each of us walked around the house (it had a swimming pool built half inside the home and the other half outside...very distinctive).

All of us made our way to the cars...except little Markie. He liked to investigate his surroundings bringing him behind us for a little ways. Unbelievable...as he was passing between the parked cars (our car and our friends) the brakes of our friend's car released and Mark was crushed between the two cars. I picked him up but he went limp over my shoulder. My husband carried him to the fence and sat there. The neurosurgeon said: "don't you think we should take him to the emergency room." We sped away with him to the ER. I asked my husband 'will he live'...no answer...I was pushed out of the ER, but I rushed back in as Mark was turning blue and life slipped slowly away.

Even now as I speak my heart is overcome with dreadful pain. All night the words "The Lord is my Shepherd—I shall not want" echoed over and over again...until the morning brought clear singing of the birds...never were their sound so beautiful and hardy. The hours that followed were like walking through a dream. I never felt so stone-like...nothing seemed to penetrate my being. Somehow God got through to let me know I had a husband and other children to console. All the questions asked by the children and loved ones were almost more than I could bear. As I look back it was God that held me together...The next few days and the funeral are like a dream now...Every time I have ridden in a limousine I never ride without remembering the moment I was picked up for the last time with my little boy. It was a blessing God gave us another child (Louis) a few months later. I was not eating, but the pregnancy encouraged me not to harm a gift from God.   One would want to ask how I ever got through the scene of such a death of a child. It is only with God's constant watch care, the love of my husband and children *and* wanting to help others be able to know that with God in their lives...*everything is possible. Yes, the scene of that early evening never leaves, but God always holds me together.* This is another time for thank-fullness...ALL the folk that came to my rescue...it is true...after the funeral one seems so alone to fight a battle of never ending terror. The people God sent to me during this falling rain gave me new words of strength and comfort. At the time, nothing seemed to break through my brick wall. I fell victim to wanting some aloneness everyday...so off to the cemetery...once there...crying mournfully! I shall never ever forget that sound as it echoed far beyond my ears to time and space.

Walking slowly forward searching for anything that would take away my constant mental pain. I tried every thought that could possible take me away from tracing the last hours before and after the death occurred. Nothing worked.

Soon I realized I was with child. That was a blessing...I needed to eat...and eat healthily. I continued to tell myself maybe this pregnancy was the child I lost, but soon I had to tell myself...that was not good thinking. We were so thrilled when a beautiful healthy baby was born...he, Louis was a beautiful joy to our broken family.

Time passed and yes, we had another tragedy...our house burned to the ground. Had we not lost our little Markie first, the house would have been more horrible than it was...meaning...nothing is as terrible as the death of a loved one...especially watching a child crushed to death. We lived above the Los Angeles Fairgrounds. Some children were playing with some paper plates. It was very windy...why they were trying to burn them remains to be known. The wind caught them and blew them right up into our hills and also some young boys on motorcycles were starting fires in the valleys of our hills which eventually came like a fire ball into the path of our house and continued on, doing all the damage that could be possibly done...Again folk quickly came to our rescue. My husband, son and daughter were flying home from a trip. The children looked down from the plane as they were approaching Brackett Field, where our plane was housed, and said: "daddy, our house has burned down." My husband said: "that is not funny children"...then he realized by their terror that they were not kidding. By this time he too had viewed all they said. Upon reaching our premises, and seeing the house was gone...they panicked, wondering if I and our little Louis were burned along with the house. Soon, they were able to contact me via the "Medical Exchange." This was another serious shock in our lives. By this time, one does wonder what God is trying to tell us. It takes years to understand the meaning of such tragic circumstances. I suppose, even though the mind is inclined to linger in the tragedy, one eventually has to take forward steps. Personally, without a doubt, I was, am scarred for life. I can honestly say, however, that God does help us to walk bravely on in the crowd to notice how others too have been taken in struggles. One can't become blind to the reality of how life is to all mankind. I love what John Quincy Adams once said to a friend after he had a stroke: "I inhabit a weak, frail, decayed tenement ...battered by the wind and broken by the storms, and, from all I can learn, the landlord does not intend to repair." You see, there are so many others battered and broken by the storms of life...some suffering far beyond imagination, but still leaving a path of hope and peace.

Sometimes I find it very difficult to find a resting place at nighttime when trying to fall asleep. As I say my prayers I start thinking about those in far away places...places of unrest due to disasters, harsh conditions and some not knowing where a loved one is...maybe being in undercover and suffering abuse of some sort. I keep praying for a way of escape for them or being exposed. Also all the little animals under extreme torture by the hands of criminals...I am so broken.

God has left us with many promises that carry us through, but as long as sin is with us we will be subjected to the storms of life. I do love what Jesus said after the flood: "Seedtime and harvest, cold and winter, day and night will never cease".

It wasn't too long after our house was destroyed that an earthquake struck. We were living in a house not too far from where our house burned down and yes, things got tossed and broken. We were blessed that none of us were injured, including my visiting mother from Michigan. Living close by to our burned property made it very convenient to monitor each step of the way as our new home was being built.

It seemed the evil forces had not given up on us yet...the Hong Kong flu hit us hard...I stayed without any symptoms until all family members shared their turns. By now we were accustomed to not so good surprises. One learns lessons so quickly through trial and also becomes a stronger leader with God's wisdom and grace. Through all my times of disruptions, the brief encounters with many different types of people have left their mark...I have to admit that without alluding at length I am a more experienced person to be able to understand and appreciate the world around me than would never have been imagined. I wish all those folk that left so many wonderful imprints were around today, so I could give them words of appreciation and sweet hugs!

I am away from home just now, and I have no Wi-Fi where I am staying...I want to take the time and thoughtfulness to thank the most wonderful neighbors (Susan and Harry) for their sweet kindness and support. Isn't it delightful that God provides openings to closed doors. These folk have taught me so much about what is important and what can wait AND the beauty of being there for others. And of course my trip would not be possible without the sharing of home and sweetness of my Granddaughter and Grandson-in-law. It is always somewhat difficult when interrupting schedules of those that provide place and time, but I can truthfully say I never felt to be a burden...in fact I only felt the joy of their hearts the whole time of my visit. I think that is incredible, especially in this day and age.

Soon our new house was completed and the dear soul that helped with the interior decorating of our house before the fire, returned once again to share her lovely talents...assisting us until all rooms were beautifully decorated. I loved the way we chose to do my bathroom...a Sunken built in ornate tub and red ornate wall paper. I shall never forget the lovely Green baby grand piano my husband got for me and how he had a platform built for it and had the wall behind the piano papered with Marie Antoinette. Everything inside and outside was very Grecian...including a gorgeous red velvet sofa. We had an architect (German) for our outside design...what a genius he was...he loved Grecian statues and Corinthian columns...his work was so spectacular. He helped design Caesars palace in Las Vegas. This all was wonderful, but nothing took away our life-time broken hearts.

Our child's death eventually broke up a happy home...not because we fell out of love, but we couldn't keep up with the overwhelming loss we suffered. The children not only suffered the loss of their sweet little brother, but now again had to bear another heavy burden. Oh, if only I had the insight then that I possess today. I am so blessed to have children that love me deeply in spite of my weaknesses and feverish ways. Today, I know the pain of losses. I not only have Mark to mourn but my husband is no longer upon this earth. I miss him more each day and realize more and more just how much I loved this man. I respected him and cherish all the wonderful memories we created while dating, through marriage and with our dear little family. I, soon to be 95 know what it is like to lose...not only my child and husband, but all my loved ones, I am the only one left, other than nieces and nephews and 3 cousins. I have many cousins down the line, which I so appreciate, but unfortunately don't have the privilege of being around them.

As I sit upon my chair and wait upon my next words, I can't help but feel the comfort for all my past memories. What an awesome God in spite of all my losses.

My husband and I both remarried, but not really feeling the same as when we were together as a family. Many sad things came about, but all the while God was watching closely over us during these times of grief and uncertainty. Storms, winds, rain and snow passed us by many times before we reached a destination of togetherness again.

I so many times feel like a feather in the wind...floating...wondering and always looking for ways to escape from things of the past. And some things that I would love to correct, but no one is around anymore to say I am sorry to. We should be quick to make all things right as soon as possible ... but maybe we don't see the light until much later. As time marches on I am loving more and more deeply and understanding the meaning of an agape love...which so many of us don't even cherish because it fails to catch our attention. I just want so much to be God's witness not only in word but in performance.

So many days have lapsed since writing...I have been very much caught up in preparing my apartment for renovations. I have never done this before...it feels like I am moving out, and actually I would prefer it that way. I have decided to be kind and loving for all concerned. In doing so I know I have to pray much and see that I see all the good being done for my convenience and enjoyment. It is so healing knowing that someone's life has been comforted by my attitude of good faith. I think of my mother during these times. She would always say: "make folk feel good, but always make certain what you say is honest." I had such a wonderful teacher and one of great love and respect from my mother. So many times I need to ask her something...more and more I miss all the times that God gave us. I strongly urge all my readers to take time to listen to your mother's wisdom and draw in all that love given, for one day it will not be there and life will take on a new meaning all together.

More time has slipped away, but today has been beautiful. It is nearing Spring...I love just before Spring comes upon us. Returning from the big city of Grand Rapids I couldn't help but feel the warmth of sunshine through my car window and gaze upon the passing trees. I could tell they were getting ready to spring forth the buds of soon opening beauty. Upon arriving home I quickly made rounds of residents in my building that have had illnesses or just simply are lonely. I consider at my age how privileged I am to have the mobility and energy to help cheer those that are not so privileged. I thank Jesus everyday for honoring me with all talents given me through all these years. I am reminded over and over again to continue a path of healthy living. I am not my own. I belong to God and humanity. I love to start my day with prayer and study of God's word that I can better fulfill my purpose in a spiritual way. My son and I finish the day with a study of one chapter from the Bible each evening...sometimes it is difficult to understand all that is written, but it is good that God has His shepherds out there to help bring us better understanding. Also God has blessed my son with much insight. It is so important to know how much we are blessed with children that love walking with our sweet Lord. Bringing your children up knowing God will forever bring comfort and deeper wisdom that otherwise would not have existed.

Before I continue more on my journey I have to stop here to make known how my heart gets broken almost daily as I listen and counsel folk in mental pain as well as physical. Both affect the other. Counseling is far from joyful moments, but the joy comes when our ears and arms can help others to find a more peaceful walk. Today leaves me with a troubled heart...nothing was really settled...but maybe a more realistic version of what needs to happen to come to fruition. I find that there are so many folk suffering from situations that take away from their wellbeing. Trying to bring comfort and solutions to these folk is an everlasting struggle. As a counselor we are taught to not get carried away with the feelings of our subjects. If one is a true Christian, that is impossible! But, yes, we must be strong and able to accept the reality that all things cannot be solved without time and effort AND the willingness of those involved. What I am trying to say...this is a difficult time in which we are living, which will leave us most of the time broken for all we attempt to help. Folk need to read in the psalms. It is full of wisdom, especially for to-day...I love how much our Heavenly Father is always there to comfort and protect His own.

Psalm 27:4...*One thing have I desired of the LORD, that will I seek after; that I may dwell in the house of the LORD all the days of my life, to be behold the beauty of the LORD, and to enquire in His temple...*

Chapter 5

Walking the Lonely Trail

Time after the loss of our beloved son didn't come without yearnings...though God walks us through these hours of severe mental agony life never feels the same...it is very difficult to explain the difference. Folk are kind and loving, but unless you have shared the experience you'll never know nor feel the heart-aches of the grieving. At these times we have to navigate pretty much on our own.

My husband and I tried to feed comfort to the other, but it just could not be done. He had the responsibility of delivering babies and I had children to love and care for.

Our son William was accepted in the California Boy's Choir...which was an incredible experience. Not only did he do the choir but as a result, he performed at the Los Angeles Music Center...singing and acting with the New York City Opera and Ballet. We were thrown in with the opera and ballet stars. One ballerina became our lifelong friend. I was asked to join in the chorus and do some ballet...perhaps best that did not happen for reasons best unsaid. Don't we all have un-published chapters in our world of living....hmmm! The most wonder of all was meeting and talking with Beverly Sills. Most of you have been blessed by her beautiful singing voice. I shall never forget the kindness of these folk and will always be grateful for their humility in giving me some of their attention.

During this time my husband and I were growing more and more apart...we somehow could not seem to work together in our healing process of our little boy's death. He became very devoted to his calling while I was spending time with the children and their activities. Debra also was doing some devoted ice skating at the time of William's music demands so I joined her to do some figure skating. Louis was just thankful to have time with his father, mother and siblings, but found ways to find new adventures. He loved singing some of my opera pieces with me...he has a beautiful voice, but never desired to travel the road of fame...at least in the vocal world. We as a family made some sweet trips together, which was a good thing at this time to help with our healing. Because the others were occupied at the time, Louis and I made a few trips driving across the U.S.. We have many precious memories that remain with us to this day. Oh, how we long to retrieve some of those moments to do some things differently...

Before I continue the above walk I need to bring some sweet news to you...

TODAY IS MARCH 24 2024...my 95th year of living. I'm unbelievably at loss of words...Never in years of long ago did I picture myself walking this earth at 95!!! Not only am I of much age, but God has blessed me with good health, loving children and grandchildren, other loved ones, friends of all walks of life AND the ability to be there to bring comfort, joy and assistance to those who do not have the privileges of my being. My son William came from Boston to be with me and of course I still have my son Louis with me. William took me to see a live performance of the Metropolitan Opera of New York at a cinema near by. The opera was Romeo and Juliet. William and I both agree there is no other opera music as beautiful as ROMEO AND JULIET. The week was full of fun and laughter...yes, moments of sad reminiscing, but lots of walking, tennis, ping pong, throwing baskets, trips to the country and nights of movies and sharing with others. I am one of the most blessed people walking this earth. Why can I say this...because I have had the Lord in my life since birth and parents and grandparents that had walked with the Lord since their birth also. If I can say anything to enlighten the hearts of man and encourage your giving to your fellowman, it would be to keep a kind loving attitude and be grateful for all things. If only we can know that God sees the end from the beginning our lives would be much more easily perfected into understanding all things. The world about us is growing more dark with each passing day, but we have a powerful God that is with us always...our faith and trust in our Heavenly Father will carry us through each step of the way. Never give in to satan's deceptions. God is the Creator and Author of ALL things...I love reading in the psalms. They are full of trust and praise, faith and hope and so much love from the author. They also teach us to be sorry for sin, and thankful for God's loyalty. I especially love how David describes God's faithfulness during times of trouble. Such beautiful words from David that reaches deep in our souls! Of course all the Bible is beautifully written. The story of Joseph stays with me always...so much depth, and planned outcome for the future. To me, this is one of the greatest stories ever told. It gives us hope and encouragement during all times.

I want to thank all folk reading this book that was with me on my 95th for all their trust and belief in me as a human being. For their tender loving care and love...For making this day one of the most beautiful of all times. It is my prayer that God will bless my continued walk and writing of these pages to a sweet audience that can be benefitted by the story of my journey.

So life traveled down lonely difficult roads as my husband and I journeyed apart for a time. There were many stories to be told, but not really to one's enjoyment. There were men knocking at my door, which always made me wonder why they were there. I would love to think it was because I was special or that they felt I needed some support during these times of break-up and the loss of my precious child. I did meet some folk of kind concern and yes, some that were perhaps there for "their" benefit. I am sorry to say that some married doctors offered to divorce and marry me. I am thankful that God taught me to know we cannot have happiness at the expense of others unhappiness. Both my ex-husband and I did remarry which didn't bring the happiness that each of us knew in the past. Grass is not greener on the other side of the fence...it only fades and withers as the winds and storms toss it about. The children suffer during these times. I am so grateful that my/our children were given the wisdom to eventually forgive we parents for our weaknesses and then become awesome loving and beautiful human beings. I have learned so much from each child...God really blessed them with insight, wisdom and hearts full of love and understanding. There were times when it hurt to listen to some of their times cast to the wind while we, the parents were finding ourselves. And, yes, there are some of those experiences that leave me with horrible brokenness...not because of their lack of enthusiasm and kindness, but rather my failure to understand life as it should be.

I WOULD LIKE TO INCLUDE A PAPER
MY YOUNG SON WILLIAM
WROTE FOR A CLASS ASSIGNMENT...

My Life Story by Billy Lubke

I was born on 12/4/1960 in Arizona at the Air Force base.

When I was 2 months old we traveled from Arizona to Michigan.

I lived there for about 2 1/2 years then we took a long trip to California because my dad did not like the snow. We first lived in Claremont. Then one night my dad came home and said he bought a house in Ganesha Hills.

We lived there for a few years then our troubles began. First my brother died when we were looking at a new house. He was smashed between two cars. Then on 9/28/70 we were coming back from Arizona , we had gone there to visit...well, when we got back we found that our house burned down.

My mom said she was working at her desk and my brother came in and said there was a fire that fire didn't do anything but my mom sent my brother to the baby sitter. Well when she got back the fire was over but then all of a sudden at the other end of the hill the fire started again by some teenagers on a motorcycle well by this time my mother was in the bathroom getting reddy to go somewhere but her conscience was bothering her so she ran to the kitchen to see what was a matter by that time the fire was up by the house so she ran back to finish dressing, then she ran down the hill but she forgot her keys but anyway there was fire all around the car. Then some teenagers drove around and picked her up in there car.

So that night when we got home we went to spend the night at somebody else's house.

Then we found a house in Ganesha Hills until we built our house again.

But when the summer came we had fun in Michigan.

We traveled from Michigan to California. We stopped at a lot of places along the way. Our first attraction was the four heads of George Washington, Thomas Jefferson, Abraham Lincoln and Teddy Roosevelt.

Then when we got in Jackson Hole Wyoming we went to the Tramway.

The place where we stayed had a swimming pool that was 96 degrees.

When we got to California my relatives stayed at a trailer camp. They saw our house and how it had gained progress. They only stayed a couple weeks then they went home.

Now we have rebuilt our house but we haven't finished the outside yet. And that's the story of my life.

The man I did marry was a dentist with many talents...but it soon became clear that this marriage was not the answer to happiness...he was wonderful in his own way, but somehow it did not remove the love I left behind for the father of our children, nor help erase the pain of the beloved child brutally snatched away. This marriage did bring a wonderful person in my life...called "Papa". He was so talented with words and brilliant understanding. At the end of his life he tenderly took me aside and said: "you have reached your mountaintop through many dark valleys...now God is ready for you to bless the world." Even today I feel the chills up and down my spine as I put these words upon these pages. I feel I had just begun.

God, however, handles my steps forward and has always done so from the moment of birth. Papa always drew a burning candle at the end of his letters to me:

Again I was left to wander in a path of struggles. I have so many regrets, yet so many people to cheer for all their devotion and sacrifices they made to my way of a better life.

During these dark hours I had been putting together words that later became a book and I also was asked to do a gospel recording. I received International Angel Awards for both of them. I was very humbled by such honor and hopefully gained some courage to share some wisdom that God was giving me with those that were seeking some encouragement for some of their failures and hardships that exposed them to some very troubling times. I had been asked to do some gospel con-certs...traveling to places around and out of the country. I even found time to finish my degree in Psychology in Maine...all the teachers there were exceptional, but one of the sisters made her way into my heart and it stayed until her death. Also one of my professors made my life so sweet by his kind loving devo-tion to see that I accomplished what I set out to achieve. No matter where I was in my schooling I always minored in Music and took some courses in tennis. How blessed I was. I even did some journeys across America all by myself. You see, back then, it was quite safe, for the most, to be alone in travels and such. Today, I don't feel safe walking down side streets. Age doesn't matter anymore to the evil ones. It is a time to put all our trust in the mighty One and think upon who God really is...never to lose sight of His power, love, compassion and His watch care over us.

There were times of severe difficulties with my daughter

Ramona...I thank the Lord that she lived through these horrible times of upset...even though the hurt was unbearable at times for all of us, she did give me some tender, very sweet moments of comfort and warmth, never to be forgotten. She had many wonderful goals ahead of her, but somehow they were whisked away when death nearly claimed her. Today, her sweetness abides, but her physical health does not permit any major activity. Regardless of all circumstances...a child is always dear to a parent's heart.

There are always concerns after a divorce in raising children, but I am happy to say that each child found a way of bringing love, comfort, joy, peace and learning to us and to all they touched and touch so far in their journey. One completed her course in Occupational Therapy, another became a Urologist and the youngest one became an awesome Accountant.

Somewhere in my youth or childhood, I must have done something good for God to have blessed me with magnificent people and loved ones in my journey. I sometimes just sit surrounded by God's beauty and think about all the wonderful moments given me and all the unbelievable words spoken in my behalf. I am so thankful, that in spite of all my low times, God was *always* there to help me become a little more charming and knowledgeable in my way of life. Because of my deep love for Him and knowing how He forgave me on the cross I find myself being very tender when one asks for forgiveness. In fact, how any of us could not forgive makes me shed tears for those that are on an unforgivable journey.

Tonight, my son and I have much of the apartment packed for renovations...It reminds me of "Grapes of Wrath". I find it very difficult to pack for such occasions. Meaning it is very hard to pack for temporary reasons. At times such as these God helps us to grow and learn more about how to build a more effective way of treating folk under these circumstances. I am thankful that God gives me many chances to grow and become more wise in my walk of life.

My days are long sometimes, but nighttime seems to be mine...a time to reflect...a time to compose and see things that lack of time during the daytime hours steal from me. Tonight I am taken back to R.E.Novak...he loved to write beautiful deep words to me or that could include anyone:

"I cannot show you what you cannot see.
I cannot will a life for you, if you will it not to be.

My dream for you can never be,
If you choose me or you , but not we.

My path leads me in a way from which I dare not stray,
I would walk with you hand in hand
    so you will not lose your way.

I see a path that leads beyond the hill. Its end I cannot see,
Yet I travel it gladly for I know the best is yet to be.

If you choose a different path and another hand to hold,
I pray your journey, be it long or short, keeps you in the fold.

We have traveled far, you and I, and yet there comes a day
When my hand will be gone but my path traveled with you,
    for so long, is here to stay.

It makes me think...for those who have known my heart, they alone will know the joy of each item I touched and the treasure will live again in their heart as it lives in mine.

Chapter 6

My Sweet Lord

Long, long ago, back in the 1930's I heard the voice of my mother, calling out for us children to end our evening play and come in to prepare ourselves for bed and evening worship. How sweet it was to have a mother that cared about our love for Jesus. As you recall our father was killed early in our lives, which made it very difficult for a mother to carry out all the responsibilities placed upon her without a husband and father. How she found the time for extra special times to keep us in tune with heaven above, remains still to be a great mystery.

Again I was blessed at my early age to feel the beauty of my sweet Lord while helping out my sister with her children. I shall cherish forever that early contact with God and His awesome Kingdom by the Christ-like teachers, that day after day lived their love for God and never missed a chance to share their Bible knowledge with us students. It is indescribable how deeply and beautifully touched I was during those unforgettable years.

It is so inspiring for children and youth to be involved with things in life that will guide their path forward to a happy fulfilling ending. Of course all of us will always be subjected to the negative and times of great disappointment...but with a good foundation from early youth, life will be much easier to achieve our goals and become better citizens here and in the earth made new.

As I traveled throughout high school and college I seemed to have enough energy and motivation to encourage others in the walk that helped me be happier and content. It wasn't until more serious dating and relationships became more difficult to stay on the same path. Meaning...others seemed to slowly pull me from my wonderful teachings. I want to strongly say--at no time was I truly happy walking the road of unknown ending. Today, I am so grateful that no matter how much I strayed at times from my previous teachings and practices, God was always there to bring me back. Our God is such a loving, awesome God. He knows our hearts and will never let us get lost forever in our weaknesses.

Parents, never forget...what you do and teach your young children will stay with them through all times...meaning should they take detours, God will be watching over them and bring them back to a peaceful and loving Christ-like life!

Oh, how much I long to inspire parents or anyone responsible for the growth of a child to be knowledgeable in the hereafter in a child's grown-up life. In counseling many a youth I am so disheartened as I hear their longing to know the true love and affection of a parent. So many children never had the blessing of a loving parent. So many dramatic stories I could tell...maybe not as epic as you think, but still it is "their life-time heartache." How many times did their cry for approval or to hear "I love you son" or "I love you daughter" shout out quietly......

Many children travel far before they learn who God really is. Yes, God does have set rules and he does want us to be perfect...but no man is without sin...so how do we reconcile these facts. God is our sinless Example of the power we can claim through faith in Him...Jesus died for our sins, paying our penalty required to reconcile us to God. We need not force our children to see God as a harsh God...He died for us while we were yet sinners. We as parents should show the love of God through nature and a loving spirit toward our children and all humanity.

Our journey in this life is not measured by hours, days, or years, but by the sweet things we scatter about our path. Standing tall to be seen, thinking our life is important...for it is not...our journey here is short...it's our sweet spirit that lives on and on forever in the hearts of those who loved us.

I love what Robert E. Novak once said to me; "We mortals know for a Garden of Eden to exist it must have a Tree of Knowledge and a Deceiver. Since we are human, living daily with our own personal problems, we do vacillate between the two. This Spiritual gene, because of its nature must choose which path to follow.

Not too long ago I was faced with opportunities that would raise me high...It is these times in time that we really need to know things such as above I speak of. When we get to heaven we will be so grateful for all the times our Heavenly Father stood between us and disaster. Aren't you thankful for all the times that God intercedes to save us from horrible outcomes. We have a wonderful loving God. So many times we think it is cruel how things turned out...I have lived long enough and been blessed with how some things were made plain at a later time in my life. I got on my knees and thanked God over and over again. Yes, we don't always see the outcome, but with complete faith in God we can be at peace knowing that *all things do work together for good.*

One of the greatest marvels and comforts in my life is that the same librarian that served my mother is still serving me in that same library...(dating back 50 years). Also it thrills my soul that my cousin, just 5 years younger than I, still goes to this library every few days to check out several books. For those that read my above comments, I know you can't help but be thankful that life can be so full of wonderful happenings, knowing that one day you could be privy to the same. I could write a huge book just with "THANKS" to our sweet Lord...as you also could do the same.

It wasn't too long ago a dear person was telling me about how she had lost several children...my heart breaks every time I think about how she could ever recover from such devastating losses. Her faith and love of God is unbelievable. I forever am amazed, deeply touched and comforted at the same time. Though such frequency of heartaches give me pauses...in the end God has given me greater strength and courage to serve all that are broken in a more peaceful manner.

So many times in our lifetime I am sure all of us have picked up the phone to learn of someone's great tragedy. We need to be so careful at those moments that we ask God for the most comforting words that will bring them close to our sweet Lord...Life is very precious and oh how we need to soften our hearts that we can make the difference between dark or light in lives. We must take care of ourselves in the best way we know how...folk need us...they need the Lord and we must be here to help guide them in that direction.

A few days ago a very sweet young student that just graduated from Optometry said: "I think I have been fortunate enough in my life that any time something got dark, hard or difficult I always had the trust in knowing God would come through no matter what, it was just a matter of waiting for His timing." This was such a touching moment to hear such beautiful words. I love the youth...they keep all of us alive and full of joy.

I love when folk come to me with stories that have sweet endings. It is not always that way, but God has His reasons. One day all things will be made plain. Until, we must keep the faith.

Some years back one of my nieces brought to my attention how she had felt hopeless when her dad was going through some health issues and passed away. She felt loneliness like never before. She said: "I faced parts of myself I didn't like and tried to ignore for many years prior. As time has gone on I've made new connections that brought support and sought healing in all aspects of my life...mind, body and spirit. So the biggest hole in my life also filled me in other ways. This has happened over years. I'm grateful I get the opportunity to look back and see that growth. I would say the person I am today I couldn't imagine being at the point he died. I was filled with so much anger and now, the opposite. I feel filled with so much love even despite difficult." Our sweet Lord gives many blessings...even in the darkest moments of our lives.

Not just because of my degree in Psychology do many flock to be comforted, but because of my God-given willingness. I do love mankind with such a passion...I give God the credit for that love and thank Him every day for all those that can be soothed by the wisdom He supplies. Without God we are nothing...with Him miracles can be performed!

I love how David in the psalms writes such beautiful words...not only to give hope but his personal words about how the pastures are clothed with flocks, the valleys also are covered over with corn...they shout for joy and sing. He says: "Give us help O Lord...for vain is the help of man." God stills the music of the sea, the noise of the waves and the tumult of the people." Yet there is healing in the music of the sea...its waves and the glory of its beauty to the eye.

The last few days have been full of needs to neighbors, some students and even some military. It seems the earth is groaning with hurt and pain from unusual causes. I find without God in my life I would be helpless in bringing comfort and hope to all that knock at my door. We know that the closer we get to the end of time things will increasingly change all around us. This is a time for stability as never before. AND God is the only one that can make that happen in our lives. There are some folk that have been plagued with unknown physical conditions. As wonderful as the medical profession is, sometimes they cannot come up with good solutions or treatment. This is when my heart fails me sometimes for the lack of comforting words. I will say, I am so blessed to have had a Christian background, otherwise there would be no way to rescue the perishing from their fright and the unknown.

In the following words I want to share some experiences from those that have had dark valleys, but with God's grace they found themselves with ways to see beyond their darkness. Some didn't find the peace they hoped for, but...with their complete trust in God are walking in the path of sweet belief of a better tomorrow. We don't or we won't always have a sweet ending. There are times when God sort of leaves us hanging, so to speak. That is when we need to trust knowing that God is with us through all times and will eventually make all things sweet. *We do have a sweet Lord...*

Before I continue with the above experiences I set out to relate to you I need to share a frightening moment that took me by surprise a few days ago. My son was traveling across the upper U. S. on his BMW motorcycle enjoying all the lovely places of interest. I had been following him on my phone location when all of a sudden the location stopped. During this time I prayed and asked God to give me peace. At first I was at peace knowing God was watching over him but as time passed away I seemed to lose my faith.   Five hours, six hours, seven hours, eight hours...and finally twenty hours plus showed on my location...no movement!!! I have always been able to calm the storm in other folks lives during uncertain times, but now I realize I didn't have a true sense to how they were really feeling at the time of their discomfort. Yes, the location finally picked up again and I later learned that there was no service . I suspected that, but that didn't seem to comfort me at the time. I thanked Jesus so much and I can't tell you the wonderful peace that swept over me as I saw the movement of the photo of my son moving along rapidly. There are times when things don't turn out so sweetly, but God sure does teach us many lessons during happenings such as this. I know the terrible feeling when horrible endings occur...the loss of my child. As I have expressed the path to recovery is a long journey.

Yesterday, a friend called that had finished reading my book: "F Sharp #" telling me how much the words are helping her get through a time of despair...how dark her valley has been thinking life would never be sweet again. God is bringing her through.

Since my last writings upon these pages so many have called, stopped in or text me about how dark their valley is. There are so many stories of deep pain, hurt or wondering how anything good will come at the end of their present journey. We do know that God is with us always. While waiting in a room provided for us while new carpet was installed in our apartment building I happened upon a young woman sobbing mournfully...upon asking her what was wrong she said she was crying at the unexpected loss of her daughter a few weeks ago. She said I cry like this everyday. There are no words at times like this. One can only give a strong hug and say "I am so sorry." I went to the cemetery every day for three months after the loss of my young son. It was a place up in the hills where I could mournfully cry without having to explain to anyone...only the hills, mountains and open air were there to hear me. Yes, God heard. I can still hear that horrifying sound of my cry...Let us all be more aware to the hidden sorrow of others. Some can share, others find it too earth shaking to let go of their deep sorrows.

There are so many young folk going through troubled relationships...I try to comfort them by saying: "you can't go wrong by asking for God's will to be done." That way we know we are safe in that God's way is the best way. He keeps us from getting more hurt by listening to His voice.

1 Peter 5:10, 11...But the God of all grace, who hath called us unto His eternal glory by Christ Jesus, after that ye have suffered a while, make you perfect, stablish, strengthen, settle you. To Him be glory and dominion for ever and ever. Amen.

Some time ago a young woman found herself pregnant with child...she married because of, but wasn't really in love with the father of the baby. Unfortunately more babies were born and trial after trial found her deeper in hurt and pain. She didn't have God in her life and things got very dark. The husband was not being kind and loving and just when she thought there was no future happiness she found God...yes, she had to move on out of that marriage. She eventually remarried and now has several wonderful grandchildren. It isn't always best to go into something because of circumstances, but we must trust God to help us make sensible decisions. I am sure one learns many lessons during dark valleys which prepare us for more difficult situations in life that make us more resilient. Each time we are broken or travel a road of uncertainty we become stronger in the support of others' brokenness.

I could go on with many circumstances of disappointment and how God brought them through to a better place. We must be very grateful for all the folk that help us get through dark valleys. *We must never forget that without the help of others we could never accomplish anything in this life. And let us not forget to praise God and to bless the Lord, O my soul!*

Yes, MY SWEET LORD will always be my sweet Lord until I am no more...

Chapter 7

Still Climbing

Kids

These dear little faces tell a huge story...some sweet, some so sad. Together we shared many joys and sorrows.

As God continued my walk of faith I entered the world of

the unknown. I ventured into the college doors again to further my education. It was there I found ways and people to soften and encourage a more positive outlook. Teachers and students alike gave me lasting inspiration that yet today scatters sunshine to me and those that share my path.

Writing my first book, and recording my CD not only brought the "International Angel Awards" but brought a very special person in my life that has been one of my greatest inspirations and my forever close friend. I have other close male friends that are my sweetest of joys. I am SO thankful for all they have done and do to make everyday of my life one of joy and inspiration.

The gospel concerts throughout many states and two countries along with the "Joseph Story" I did in several Michigan cities reach far into the hearts of many. I am blessed many a time not only with the beautiful memories, but with spoken memories of others that never forget the beauty that God gave us during those times of performance. I thank everyone for all their support and perseverance in being a part of my gospel singing and the "Joseph Story".

Today I am thinking back to the time my cousin and I built a small shack so we could put together the balsam wood airplanes...and believe it or not...we both became pilots. My cousin flew for Merv Griffin. I am so thankful for this sweet cousin. He no longer is with us, but oh, the wonderful memories he leaves behind.

I made several trips across the country with my sons that forever bring me thanks for their love and caring.

I have been given several trips to Alaska, California and Florida thanks to my dear children and grandchildren.

I miss living in California...it was there and Washington where I was introduced to the beauty of the majestic mountains, forests and ocean...today my life is filled with memories of unspeakable beauty. I love God's awesome creation and wonderful goodness. My whole life has been shared with my Heavenly Father. I can't imagine how one can live a life without His presence in their world.

The light of the afternoon brings the beauty of the evening...God does not leave us without the beauty of one that lives by the side of the road. So many times as a young girl I got to sit on the porch with grandparents to feel the full beauty and awe of a sunset. Not too many folk are with me today that walked with me so many years ago. We need to cherish all the moments given to us with loved ones, and other folk. Do you realize at this very moment God is giving us something special to put in our hall of memories? He does not waste our time, but increases the value of every single moment we give to Him to fill. Oh that we not give our time and energy to foolishness...**we have so little time to receive and to give away...let us use every word and action to the glory of our Heavenly Father.**

The children above, as I said before, have grown beautifully, but not without the pain and hurt of climbing to higher ground. Oh, how I love these dear children from God. My life has been changed beyond all understanding. All of us need to thank our wonderful Lord and parents for the caring and never ending support and prayers in our behalf. I don't think we have adequate pictures in our mind of all the love that led us through all the dark valleys nor the sweet times.

Sometimes the walls close in on us...it is during these times that God speaks more clearly and prepares us for all that be before us. We mustn't be overwhelmed for all that is happening just now...God has His eye upon every beating heart. He is there to touch every soul with the force of His splendid character if they so desire. I feel we should get to the point of loving ALL mankind and leave the not so good opinions to God alone.

LET YOUR HEART FEEL
FOR THE AFFLICTIONS
OF EVERYONE...
George Washington.

It grieves me much to put upon these pages that again I had to close another door of marriage. I want to say this, for wandering off into other fields hoping to find peace...it doesn't work. There were some times of sweetness, but for the most it only made me feel full of sorrow for the turmoil it was creating. When I divorced my husband, the father of our little boy that was killed, the divorce didn't solve anything. Eventually it only deepened our sorrow. Back in those times counseling was frowned upon. Needless to say we became the victims of poor communication. Though later on we had the joy of continuing our love and caring for each other, it never gave us the peace that would have allowed us to make a better life not only for us, but for our children had we stayed together. However, I know it is not in God's plan to look back to things that cannot be changed, but we can help others to understand there are better ways than divorce under these circumstances. Sometimes, I am flooded with regrets...we mustn't let Satan take hold of our well being, but be at peace knowing God has forgiven us, and blessings were given in spite of. The children so sweetly tell me that they were blessed by their parents love and grew to great heights though at times they had to pass through troubled waters. God is so sweet to hear the cries of all of us and bring us to a place of peace.

As I travel back in thought it gives me sweet peace when I am reminded of all my trips to Alaska, California, Germany and other countries to be with my children. It was these times that formed many special friendships and filled my soul with everlasting beauty, courage and grace. I even got to do some mountain climbing in Alaska. We should always be thankful for all memories created at these times as well as all the memories that are made during all of our mountain climbing. I am absolutely amazed that God chose to give us memories to remember life's lessons and bring us joy.

I had the wonderful privilege of living in my mother's house on a lake in Michigan for several years...I was so thrilled whenever I saw the children and grandchildren pull in the front yard. These are some of the most beautiful memories of all time. Also, my twin (Robert) would come from a town several miles away...having a twin is one of the most precious gifts God can give to one.

There were many times brothers and a sister that lived near by would surprise me with a sweet visit...siblings are one of the greatest joys that one can experience in our lifetime.

The most awesome stars at night and the beauty of early daylight never leave the thrill of my soul...I wish I could paint all my life of beauty...I would want to leave out the darkness, however, maybe it would better your understanding of the universe. As I say this, I am fully aware that I am not the only one that has had dark valleys...so please know that my heart is full of compassion knowing that I do not walk alone.

Soon my days at my mother's house had to come to an end. It took many hours of thought and searching for where to next. After much research and prayers my son William and I felt Oregon was the place to go. With the help of my nephew and other son Louis I was packed up quickly and ready for departure to a new experience. It sounds as though this was an easy decision...though seemingly exciting, I was about to say good bye to my precious Amish friends. We had become very dear to each other and I can still hear the sobbing of my dearest Sarah. I too was caught in the sadness of the moment.

The days of travel were so wonderful, but we did get to enjoy the power and magic of winter. It was surprising when our destination found us unloading in a blizzard...I thought Oregon was somewhat mild in the winter. Later on, after conversing with the long standing residents, I learned that it can be a little harsh at times in the winter months. I did some concerts there and also got to know several wonderful people. In fact, some of the great ping pong players let me be part of their weekly routine. Tennis players were few, but somehow I persuaded a few to join me on occasions. Of course when my sons came to visit I had no problem getting them out on the courts with me. I love to watch them both play tennis...they look like pros on the court, which made me shine!

They had wonderful churches there of my faith...Seventh Day Adventist. I was privileged to perform several times while being a resident there.

Around two years passed of visiting loved ones and friends,

but somehow my life seemed to change...meaning my purpose for being there no longer existed. With some hesitation I decided to pack up and leave. I do love the west and I did feel the agony of departing to a place without mountains and an ocean. Back to my roots I went. My twin had died just before my departure which gave me deep sorrow and a horrible feeling of no longer living near the one I loved so dearly. I now have witnessed the loss of so many loved ones...those most dear. It is good to have longevity but as time passes we have to say good bye to many loved ones and dear friends.

In returning I experienced some very painful times yet God brought many beautiful things. Loved ones lived near...my church families were of sweet character and I was chosen to be Minister of Music at two different churches...which I still hold position.

I have made several trips to Alaska, California, Florida and Boston. The joy of all these travels brought much beauty of nature and mental growth. Most of all, God's beautiful universe seems to exist more precious to me each day of my life. I know the world is not as we once knew it, but somehow the beauty and mystery is to be found if we only search deeply within our souls. I know my love and respect for my Heavenly Father gives me richness of thought. One of my greatest joys of late is when my son William flew me to Alaska and then he and I flew together to Seattle, then to Boston. A few days there and then off to New York by train. Back to Boston for another few days, then I was put on a plane back to Michigan. Though I have suffered several dark moments in my time...God has always been there to help me see and feel the magnificent power and beauty of His love and character. He gives me thought of outstanding gratefulness not only to Him, but to all that have helped me journey through 95 years of time.

It is my prayer that all will be inspired to look to God for your peace and understanding.

Today, I was introduced to a beautiful outstanding young thirteen year old. I cannot believe the wisdom that God has given to him. Shortly after our introduction he proceeded to tell me "I believe in God." Upon asking him what he planned to do with his future he told me that he hoped to go to college and let the Air Force pay his way and then join forces with them. In the meantime he said he was very aware of the world situation and that how he wants to help make things better by his belief in keeping things going in a positive direction.

It is with such grateful heart to always have the young in my camp. God has been so gracious in giving the young to decorate all my journey. AND, all the college students that make my life so special. They say they could not have done it without me...what they are saying is that they could have not done it without God's gift of His missionaries.

Today I cannot forget about all the songs that my son sang to me...especially on my "up in years" birthdays. The following is one of my most memorable:

HIS EYE IS ON THE SPARROW

Why should I feel discouraged,
Why should the shadows come,
Why should my heart be lonely.
And long for heav'n and home,
When Jesus is my portion,

My constant Friend is He,
His eye I on the sparrow,
And I know He watches me

I sing because I'm happy,
I sing because I'm free;
For His eye on the sparrow,
And I know He watches me.

Let not your heart be troubled,
His tender word I hear,
And resting on His goodness,
I lose my doubts and fears;
Though by the path He leadeth,
But one step I may see;
His eye is on the sparrow,
And I know He watches me.

I sing because I'm happy,
I sing because I'm free,
For His eye in on the sparrow,
And I know He watches me.

Whenever I am tempted,
Whenever clouds arise;
When songs give place to sighing,
When hope within me dies,
I draw the closer to Him,
From care He sets me free;
His eye is on the sparrow,

And I know He watches me;
His eye is on the sparrow,
And I know He watches me

I sing because I'm happy,
I sing because I'm free,
For His eye is on the sparrow,
 And I know He watches me...

I still can hear the tenderness of his voice as he sang each word to me. Oh, that all parents have special moments from their children to warm their hearts as life becomes more and more precious.

I leave this place on the mountain climb to enter my final chapters...may God bless every soul that has followed me this far up the many jagged and twisted paths.

Chapter 8

Viewing the Mountain Top

I have loved thee with an everlasting love:
Therefore with lovingkindness
have I drawn thee... (Jeremiah 31:3)

My heart is full of many thoughts of my journey from birth to now...I want to try to find some lost sweet moments that will bring you closer to me and to your Heavenly Father. I am sure as we gather sometimes for special family times or other occasions to make memories, there are things that make those times stand out allowing us to be more caring and kind. Do you remember the camp fires...laughter and story telling that never fails to come back and remind us of all that supplied us with such wonderful joy and inspiration? It also makes us a little sad as we no longer have the same opportunities today. Our loved ones have departed, yet God somehow brings others in our midst that we can never be alone.

Though there are many reasons to be happy, there are many reasons not to feel the peace that we had as youth stepping into adulthood. The times in our youth of experiencing so called disasters seem nothing today as we travel through to higher ground. Losing all grandparents, parents, siblings, husbands, a child and many friends leaves me without the once glorious feeling of family, loved ones and life long friends. It seems each day now that I am informed of dying and unexpected death. We must have a good plan and understanding to keep us safe, healthy and maintaining a sweet attitude. My mother always stressed: "If you can do something about whatever presents itself...do it, otherwise move forward in peace."

It is a time in my life where I must not concentrate on all that has been taken away, but rather focus on the needs of others. I want to be there to help others to live a better life for a better future...to make it easier as they meet the demands of the day or world. I presume I am among the higher priority of being one of outstanding people. Meaning, gifted beyond the normal to meet all the expectations of mankind in a well pre-pared manner . At my age I do find this a little humorous that God is using me in so many meticulous ways. He is such an amazing God in how He works so sweetly and skillfully with each individual. Each day I literally get called to either visit a sick person or be of comfort and supply words of encourage-ment. I am so sorry for all the stress, pain and suffering in this world that one must endure. I am thankful that God has given me a long life to still be here to help alleviate some of the problems that overwhelm so many people.

You are not alone out there...the world is full of pain and suffering. During these uncertain times I encourage everyone to keep your eyes upon your Heavenly Father...otherwise we get caught in the crossfire of darkness rather than the fact that God is still with us AND is in control. No matter how difficult things appear...God is ALWAYS aware of all that is happening.

It amazes me how many folk that seek my support have come to me recently in a moment of weakness that pushes them into intolerable agony to the point of not wanting to keep buried secrets...secrets that turned their lives into misery. I will tell you and them...nothing is too impossible with God that cannot make one whole again. The evil forces are strong, but God is stronger. I love how Philippians 2:13 assures us that it is God which worketh in us both to will and to do His good pleasure.

Today started rather early with concern...my son was on his way from Oregon on his BMV motorcycle to Idaho. I get this call of distress from him...all of a sudden he noticed that his backpack was missing. Of course, since he was on his way for off-road biking he needed that backpack. At times such as these it is very hard to stay calm and miss the lesson at the moment. I always say: "All things work together for good." Meaning, God perhaps is saving us from something that could be of danger to us, or something needs to be gained from the situation. This story ended well...he returned to his beginnings, but the backpack was not to be found there, but later it was recovered from where it fell to the ground. There are so many good lessons to be learned from negative experiences...they may not be learned at the time, but until, we are , hopefully developing patience.

Today I was blessed with a call from a dear dear friend in my Pomona days. The days we lived in the hills of Ganesha.

He was attending the seminary to become a priest. Though very devoted to what he set out to do somehow after a year he felt he was called from God to do other things. He has been a true leader in this world...not as a priest but to all that follow in his journey. He is such a inspiring man and never fails to give me new insight into what I need to bless others. This is another to add to my collection of thankfulness. God has given me so much education through so many different methods by so many people. He has a beautiful singing voice as well as a lovely speaking voice . I taught some voice...it was so rewarding...each person has an artist within them...like each flower has its beauty. I loved to tell my students how to coordinate vocal cords, breath, posture of body and so on. And of course, water, proper sleep, and healthy eating all play an important role in any thing we choose to do in life.

Recently I have tried to console some students that are interested in reaching goals in this life. I love to direct them to Galatians 6...Especially verse 2-7. Bear ye one another's burdens, and so fulfill the law of Christ. For if a man think himself something, when he is nothing, he deceiveth himself alone, and not in another. But let every man prove his own work, and then he shall have rejoicing in himself alone, and not in another. For Every man shall bear his own burden. Let him that is taught in the word communicate unto him that teacheth in all good things. Be not deceived; God is not mocked: for whatsoever a man soweth, that shall he also reap. All of us have temptations every day of our lives, But according to James 1:12 we will one day be rewarded the crown of life, if we endure the temptations. God has promised that to all of us if we love Him.

My son is biking the back trails in Colorado...Though I sometimes fear for his safety I am blessed with all his revelations of God's wonderful nature. **He tells that no picture could ever show the depth and beauty of what his eyes can see.** We learn so much from all the unimaginable nature that God has given to us. I don't know of anything that can bring us so near and dear to our Heavenly Father. As I look intently at the world around me...how can anyone deny a God!?! It seems so many are wandering farther and farther away from beginning of time. Let us carefully examine ourselves each day that we not lose sight of all that we once had given to us at our early ages. We must always keep the faith that we not only lose our path to heaven, but that we not discourage others from staying on the pathway of life most beautiful. I am nearing the ninety-six mark...oh that God will strengthen me to be able to continue my walk of faith for every human being that needs love and encouragement. My life is in the hands of God now...He has given me so much in a long life...I want to share all that I can of myself and knowledge to better the world around me. I am thankful for all those that desire a closer connection with God and even more thankful that God has entrusted to me all that He has to bring all of you to a better place in time. Don't ever feel that you are not able to serve the Lord, for there are so many ways of being His servant. Yes, sometimes the road is rough and bumpy, but God is there to pick us up when all else fails.

I will lift up mine eyes unto the hills,
*   from whence cometh my help.*
My help cometh from the Lord, which made
*   Heaven and earth... (Psalms 121:1-2)*

My continuation of climbing won't let me forget all the folk from childhood, early grades in school, high school, youth, college, marriages, church families, neighbors, and all the folk along my path...for instance places of business, grocery stores and on and on. Sometimes I find myself sitting in the twilight upon a porch reviewing all the names that made and make my life so eventful, enjoyable, romantic, and fulfilling. I also shall never forget all the folk in choirs, orchestras and concerts-opera included. I could fill a book with all the folk that have traveled down a lonely road with me, and all others that made/make me so high spirited. I especially give thanks to all the ministers along the way that kept me close to my Heavenly Father. I love so many. I want so much to truly love. I know there are times with all of us that our love wavers when things don't work to our advantage...do you know it is at these times that I beg my Lord to forgive me and change my heart. I can see so much changing that God has to help me with before I depart this earth...oh that I will have a willing heart. I am so grateful for the folk that helped me with book writing...without them my writings would have gotten lost in the wind. Daniel, thank you! And precious Cari thank you...your books are so outstanding. I pray that folk will go to the internet to be blessed by all the talent that God has given you (Cari Haus). Cheryl...your art work brought my second book cover to great beauty.

I love how God brings to mind the things that moves us on

to a higher standard....things that we could never have imagined possible without His grace. Sometimes my climb upward found me going in circles...not knowing which path to take next...during these times there were many tears and anxiousness. It was the soft voice of Jesus later on that took my hand many times to take me out of the whirlwind. None of us deserve such love and respect that is given us. It is only through the love, kindness and compassion of a loving merciful Creator that we are blessed beyond all knowledge.

Today I was blessed with the introduction to several wonderful young women that use their talents to help folk look better and feel more confident in who they are. I was so fortunate to find them circled around me asking me so many questions. I find the older I become the more questions I am asked about how I live, what I eat, but most of all they want me to tell them what is the most important thing that I would advise for them to have a good life. The last question they ask is what was my most important season of life? Yes, powerful questions. After walking away I start feeling full of some concern...wondering, did my answers give them inspiration to a better future or could I have dug a little more deeply to satisfy their curiosity of building better characters? Maybe this moment in time will help each of you to realize how wise it is to think about these questions asked me. One day you will have the same opportunity to further develop the skills and knowledge asked of all that seek your wisdom...will you be prepared? And will you be pleased with how you managed your time and gifts given to you......

I like to tell folk how important a good attitude is, but in so doing, don't forget to tell folk that without God in your life that good attitude would not be possible. The other most asked question: "What season in your life was the most memorable?" is always difficult for me. There is so much importance that lies within all walks of existence...however, I do believe my forties was perhaps the most valuable to me. I had to learn to be happy in my sorrow after the horrible death of my little boy.

Life was never the same, but with God's grace , patience and love I was led through many years of great learning...in spite of my never to be forgotten past. Let all of us keep cognizant to all that we possible can as we build upon all that is given us...especially that we not throw away all the glory that has been given to us.

I want to bring to light here, though it may seem simple to you...do you ever forget where you left something or discover that something was accidentally lost and it was miraculously found by a sweet voice? There are many times of which I could relate these circumstances, but I want to tell you one that happened just today and then follow it with even greater joy of discovery. I was looking for my favorite little spoon that belonged to one of my grown sons. We as mothers know just how tender it is when we lose something that was preciously part of our child's early youth. I sort of let my mind go free for a spell thinking I could ask my son if he had taken it to his room or such. It wasn't long before a small voice told me exactly where it was and how it was contained. I was so excited to hear this voice and quickly went to the garbage and found the wrapped paper that it had been put in....there it was as I had remembered it. Then an hour or two later one of my granddaughter's called and as I was telling her about my happy ending to a lost spoon of my child's, she right away said: "I have lost a spoon that belonged to me as a child and somehow it got lost upon the top of the refrigerator". After I made a few suggestions and her exploring, the spoon was found. I think it is one of the most beautiful experiences how God tells us where things are. I can't help but marvel at all these simple times, just to think our Heavenly Father cares so deeply about all of our small needs and frustrations just as much as the greater ones.

In closing this chapter I would like to share some ANECDOTES of United States Presidents from my time of birth...This is one of my favorite things to do...studying anecdotes...

- Herbert Clarke Hoover...Shortly after he became president, as we know, the collapse of the stock exchange led to the Great Depression of the 1930s. This made Hoover's election promises about prosperity ring very hollow. Hoover lamented to former President Calvin Coolidge that his attempts to promote economic recovery seemed to be making little impact and that his critics were becoming increasingly angry. "You can't expect to see calves running in the field the day after you put the bull to the cows," Coolidge soothingly. "No, but I would at least expect to see contented cows," replied the unhappy president.

- Franklin Delano Roosevelt...The many details which an inaugural committee must cope with in a short time inevitably produce a few mistakes. Thus FDR, in 1937, received an invitation to his own inauguration. Through the White House social bureau he solemnly sent word that the press of official business would keep him away.

Then, relenting, he sent a further note in his own handwriting: "I have rearranged my engagements and think I may be able to go. Will know definitely January 19. F.D.R."

- Harry S. Truman...Truman had accepted the vice presidency with extreme reluctance. On April 12, 1945, he was summoned to the White House. There he was shown into Eleanor Roosevelt's sitting room and she told him gently that President Roosevelt was dead. After a moment's stunned silence, Truman asked her, "Is there anything I can do for you?" She shook her head. "Is there anything we can do for you?" she said. "For you're the one in trouble now."

- Dwight David Eisenhower...Some months after the end of his term as president, Eisenhower was asked if leaving the White House had affected his golf game, "Yes, he replied, a lot more people beat me now."

- John Fitzgerald Kennedy...Kennedy loved telling this story against himself. He said that during an election campaign his father sent him the following telegram: "Don't buy a single vote more than necessary. I'll be damned if I'm going to pay for a landslide."

- Lyndon Baines Johnson...The Senate worked hard and late when Johnson was majority leader. One weary senator complained to a colleague, "What's all the hurry? "Rome wasn't built in a Day." "No, but Lyndon Johnson wasn't foreman on that job," said the other.

- Richard Milhous Nixon...Meeting Kennedy's aide Ted Sorenson shortly after Kennedy's inaugural address, Nixon remarked that there were things in the speech that he would have liked to have said. "Do you mean the part about 'not what your country can do for you...?'" Said Sorenson. "No," he replied, "the part beginning 'I do solemnly swear...'"

• Gerald R. Ford...President Ford was playing golf with ice-hockey star Gordie Howe. At the twelfth hole, Howe conceded a two-foot putt to his distinguished opponent. Ford insisted on taking the shot—-and missed. "We won't count that one," said Howe generously. Pointing toward the reporters and Secret Service men at the edge of the green, Ford replied, "Maybe *you* won't but *they* will."

• James Earl Carter, Jr. ...With candor rare among celebrities, the president's daughter, Amy Carter, when asked by a reporter if she had any message for the children of America, answered, "No."

• Ronald Wilson Reagan...Even the democrats were impressed by Reagan's first televised budget speech, in which he used a handful of small change to illustrate the current value of the dollar. "It takes an actor to do that," admitted one of his rivals, "Carter would have emphasized all the wrong words. Ford would be fumbled and dropped the cash. Nixon would have pocketed it."

I am thankful for all these Presidents that gave their time and energy to better our country. Some may have not have pleased us as some desired, but I am sure they did the best that was given them. We must pray now that God's will, will be done in the next election. Only God knows what needs to take place to make way for His second coming.

Chapter 9

Stepping Softly

My steps are more soft and gentle now...I can see the top more vividly, yet I know I am a distance away.

As I walk this last path with my audience I feel I need to reminisce a little and also share some thoughts that come along as I find my way to the end of this book's journey.

Today as I was blessed to be asked to play the piano and sing a solo at church, I couldn't help but wonder how much longer I will be mentioned as a "living legend." I am always amazed at the devotion, love and respect that I have always been given, no matter what season of my life I have been walking through.

Something the Pastor said today really caught my attention...so many times we look at God's law as harsh but we have missed the fact that His law was given to tell us those "THOUS" are nothing more than to let us know they are promises...promises that we will not do those things. God's law is the character of our Heavenly Father...without His law think how horrible this world would be. I also was thinking today of how obedience starts in our life. It is with the parent...teaching the young child to obey...if this is not taught in early years obedience will be hated in adulthood. Which brings us to the dawning of realization...realizing that we are the sons and daughters of God...therefore wanting to please the one that created us.

We need to be ever so grateful for all that has been given us. There are so many that will never know the sweetness of life that has been given to us. My heart breaks as I think about all the people that go to bed hungry and cold and a cruel world around them. I will be so happy when Jesus breaks the skies with His coming so all this suffering can end.

I love to think back to all the sweet moments in my life as a child...Playing peacefully with dolls, walking in the woods with grandparents, going to the lakes and beaches...wading in the ocean...climbing part way up mountains. I especially loved the times with aunts and uncles, and my cousins. The most joyful of all was when grandma and my mother played the organ and piano for us children to sing hymns. As I matured I was privy to all the beautiful music by attending concerts and sometimes being part of the band and orchestra in college. If you have these privileges now, never throw away these precious moments...they will bring comfort and joy as the years claim their rightful aging. I am so blessed to have had children and their precious love and caring. I love all the times we have had together in visits, outings, and travels...and singing together. God has been so wonderful to keep them protected and full of love for me and humanity.

God has calmed many storms in my life but also given

hours, days, and years of wonderful moments that have added so much value to each experience that entered my way up the mountain.

I appreciate every person and happening in this life-time...meaning sometimes it wasn't always easy to rise above the times of hurt and pain caused by reckless actions. I early learned to "stay classy"... A young man, who still abides within my walk of life told me that ...saying "you understand what I am saying...sometimes others miss the message." God has given all of us potential...it is our duty to make it happen.

We are living in a time of unknown...stay close to God and study the Bible. We are nothing without God and would be so lonely and miserable trying to find peace without His love and mercy.

The fear of the Lord is *the beginning of wisdom...* (Proverbs 9:10)

My son arrived from Boston to take me to the little cabin on a lake in Fremont Michigan. We love spending time here. It is where the father came once a year to re-visit his childhood memories and feel the comfort of the peace that once he knew as a young boy. The sunrises and sunsets are so reminiscent of days back on the grandparents farm...Memories are not only about bringing back the long ago, but helping us to be thankful for all that a lifetime has given us.

My last thoughts of surrendering my pen and paper are those of tender feelings that keep me blessed with a beautiful closing to my final steps to you.

I will walk through my lifetime journey gathering some of

my most wonderful times of touching moments. So much will be left behind because it is impossible to remember all that touched my heart at this time. Hopefully God will open the gates and bring forth all that will touch you to stimulate deeper thought in how to capture the indispensable moments...that you will experience the beauty of life as you can with God and loved ones walking beside you. Doing this will give you a deeper understanding of how you can pass on to humanity a richer and most beautiful existence to follow...

UNFORGETTABLE MOMENTS IN TIME...

- Bible story time with our mother.
- Listening to my mother play the piano and loving all the times she couldn't wait for me to come home from college or California to sit down and play the piano for her...such a sweet mother.
- Going to the store with mummy: "If you don't need it, it is not on sale."
- Mother: "Without a good attitude life is burdensome personally and for all others."
- Mother: "Try to say something sweet to folk, but *always* tell the truth."
- I have lived beautifully and joyfully because of my mother's steadfast love and respect for God.
- All the times of family get togethers with parent, grandparents, aunties and uncles and cousins forever keeps me going with a joyful heart...
- Never to be forgotten all the times my sis "Mickey" made peanut brittle and fudge.

- A beautiful blessing was my brother Edward (Ned)...giving me sweet things, wisdom and lots of hugs.
- Brother Jack left so many years of laughter by his wonderful sense of humor and tenderness to us twins.
- My twin "Bobby" will forever bring memory of his wonderful kindness of heart, his instructions in how to be loved by mankind and especially how devotedly He served our Heavenly Father.
- Thanking Jesus for all the times I was able to row the boat across Big Stone Lake all by myself...*and* the times William (Billy) and I awakened early in the autumn to take the row boat out in the fog... longing for sounds of loons on the lake.
- Remembering the sacrifices of family, church members, doctors and pastors along the way that improve my character every day of my life.
- The love and attention from the Venden brothers in my early youth will always be one of my greatest strengths...as will the teachers, the workers and some students from all my college days. To this day, as a thirteen year old, I shall never forget these words by Morris Venden, one of my classmates at Flint Jr. Academy (only eleven years old): "Perseverance should never leave your mind". This is such an interesting phenomena in my life...it has continued to grow in my mind that hardly a day passes without this word finding its way to my head.

One day while caring for my sister-in-law, Dorothy, and sitting by each other, I happened to reach down deep in the side of the chair in which I was sitting...all of a sudden my hand told me something was there...I started pulling out twenty dollar bills until it reached the count of $80. WOW! I said: 'Dorothy, you have money in this chair.' She responded: "keep it" 'I can't...it is too much money' but to my surprise she refused to accept the money from me. God has done many extraordinary things in my life, of which I won't try to explain...I would fill up many books.

I am sure there are many sad times in our lives that never leave our minds...just know that I am aware to the ones that had most affect upon my continuance of growth, but will keep some silence that no hearts are re-broken.

A few early mornings ago a horrific storm was passing through where my son William and I were camping at a lake...I couldn't help but be reminded of all the times in my youth during storms how calm and peaceful my mother remained. To this day I am continued with many peaceful ways of life because of this awesome woman...giving us children magical steps towards a stable future.

My maternal grandmother placed within me her wonderful soft voice to a world of great possibilities. A woman of few words, but actions with dignity and grace. My paternal grandparents died before I was born...I only know that they were very dignified folk from England.

I can still see my maternal grandfather sitting in his chair of honor...He always told folk he didn't discuss religion nor politics, however...his life was packed full of stories about those who would not free him of all that he confessed not to be.

Daughter Ramona gives me never to be forgotten all her times of musical abilities and her endearing sweet love for her "Mummy."

Daughter Debra forever overflows my cup with her loving and selfless heart AND her amazing abilities with "special needs" children. She always says: "you and the boys (her brothers) have all the brains." We could never do what she does in this life so tenderly and professionally. But maybe it is good that God gave her this humble heart.

I can never get enough of my time with William, my son. From his early beginnings he has left a remarkable impression through all his journey...We never had to tell him to go to bed, when to get up, to study or be a gentleman...he was gentle and kind from his beginnings. His love for his family, children and all others is one of unspeakable understanding. God gave him a love that perhaps many will never know. I love his words: "Mother you are my priority." All my children are blessed with love of nature...William sort of stole the spotlight maybe a little more than the others. Meaning with his opera and some of his daring activities.

Mark, our dear little *Markie...gone too soon!!!* His short little life not only left a horrible emptiness but yet his sweet and rare personality created a lifetime of beautiful thought and learnings. He loved his daddy's flowers and walking around our house in the hills...

I love to hear all the moments in time of my children...how they reacted to life before and after their little brother's death and then the divorce...some so beautiful and others so sad. I am so *strongly* desiring that each of you can draw out something from this journey to the mountain top that will give you inspiration, peace and ways to encourage others. Yes, it is just one woman's journey. But aren't we here to help one another get through life's challenges without having to be alone? I want you to feel the depth of my inner love for humanity...not just a desire to put meaningless words on paper but to help you understand some things for your peacefulness.

I love to think about the times that William, after devoted study all week in Medical School, loved to leave his studies behind to go spend time with his father, especially on his sailboat and also do windsurfing. William now is being called back to windsurfing days. Like me, tennis seems to never leave my blood. William senior never departed from his love for the water and his sailboat...he sailed around the world alone...something I would fear to do, but yet there is something inside of me saying there is an excitement about being out on the waters all alone with my thoughts-just a world of water all around me and a spacious sky overhead. As I write upon this page I can feel the warmth of a gentle breeze and nothing to fear-but fear itself...

My son Louis...there is so much to be said about all the times he inspired my walk in life. I remember at the age of 13 we were driving through the San Bernardino Mountains when we had to get out to check something. From that day forward he never stops to amaze me with his insight...We have been through some troublesome times, but not without our Heavenly Father stepping in to pull us through to safety. Along with his insight God gave him a deep understanding of life and why folk react to things as they try to make it to a better place in their life. He came to stay with me supposedly to help me get settled in a new place...time seemed to pass by so quickly and perhaps no one thought I would stay on this earth as long as I have...I am sure he would have liked to return to his calling, but here he is...I am soon to be 96 and he sweetly never talks about leaving me alone...To all that live in this, my historical apartment building...he is their *hero.* I know he would not like for me to be praising him, for he is God's servant...but I have never heard him speak any negative word when he is called to duty. Like Abraham Lincoln...I believe he does his duty as he understands it...Living high in the hills of Pomona California gave all of us great appreciation for God, His wonderful display of beauty and His tenderness during one of the most difficult times of our lives. Death and Divorce can never take away all that God means to us...

I never shall forget all the words of encouragement from teachers from early grades right on through college...

All the Michigan Camp Meetings are with me as I walk the walk of faith...

Never to be forgotten...evangelist H.S.M. Richards. His "Have faith dear friend, have faith in God" will never stop ringing in my ears 'til death do I part...and the King's Heralds from especially 1937 to 1949 that were part of his ministry will never leave my beauty chambers.

The love of my devoted cousin Keith to this day fills my heart with the sweetest memories any cousin could ever possess.

There are so many forlorn that keep me alive to their needs but leave me with a brokenness difficult to explain.

I so love my special dentist...his heart is full of God's beauty in nature and gives his heart for his wonderful children...teaching them the importance of good character and love for humanity. He has devotedly sent me letter after letter written in beautiful calligraphy with so many deep words of wisdom and caring for another human being.

My heart is so full of love, gratitude, and compassion for all those that love me so dearly...and take time to show me in so many spectacular ways. My world is full of joy, happiness and love from a world of caring and devoted people. More than I ever deserve, but so thankful that my Heavenly Father chooses to give me so much in spite of my lack of worthiness. I want to leave this earth knowing that I have given all that God put me here to give...

I am SO very blessed with students that love and care for me in such a tender manner. I have been given more than I could ever imagine from them and all that has been given me. What a wonderful life has been my journey...

I remember, when losing my little nephew, going home to try and sleep. I tried so hard to comprehend death...never did that understanding arrive...then when losing my own beloved little Mark the same night fell upon me...trying beyond exhaustion to find the meaning of death...it is something that only in heaven will it be found...Passing through grandparents, parents, aunts, uncles, siblings, cousins, a child, sister-in-law, and daughter-in-law deaths, only awakens me to how much we long for heaven where we can be united once again. I am so thrilled that God has a sweet hope for us. We could never be at peace if God did not come and die for us so that one day He will come again soon and take all of us home that want to be in His kingdom.

I shall always and always be thankful for my Heavenly Melody Inc. I was permitted many places to witness for my sweet Lord.

I am so comforted when the memory of my sis and I watching Perry Como on Saturday nights rekindles in my mind. Thinking of them both brings back memories that are rare today. His voice was so heavenly...bringing such beauty to our souls. Every time I watch Michigan football the sweet memories of my sister's husband Ronnie, taking me to game after game in Ann Arbor Michigan...give me such sweet feelings...

I can't express enough how my siblings, their children, and my children used to stay up until wee hours of the morning at Mickey and Ronnie's house at the lake playing croquet. It was one of the most precious of my memories.

Oh, how I love to remember the twins, Claire and Paige, singing opera with their daddy, my son William. The girls at young ages, especially Paige, had a voice of an opera star.

I couldn't help but being filled with wonder and astonishment as Louis, my two and a half year old son in my opera rehearsal days sang my songs after I sang them.

All the years of William singing while playing his guitar most of the times we were together is one of my dearest of memories. As I mentioned before his recordings to me on my "up in years" birthdays will bring me tender feelings until the day I die.

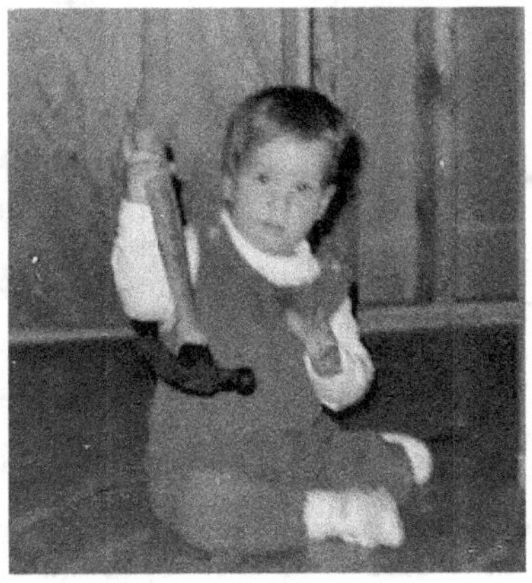

Louis

I cannot close without a few precious thoughts about my grandchildren...John always lets me know how special I am and never ceases to let me know that when he grabs me to catch me in his arms and gives the sweetest hugs ever. Tess Noel will always have that special place in my heart as I think about all the times she calls or texts to get some answers to the unknown...though very gifted

William

with wisdom she keeps a humble heart by seeking her grandmama's wisdom. Paige, my darling Paige...a very tender love for me...never was I bored when I visited her, my son and family in Alaska...she loved taking me around town and out in the snowy cold. And my adorable Claire...I can't count the times she filled my cup when in doubt or needing some inspiring words. She along with all my grandchildren are so amazing and with beautiful love surrounding them. I want to thank everyone that reads my *climb up the mountain* for your willingness to learn how you can find ways for your comfort and joy in your climbing that will also scatter beauty and happiness to all that share your journey. We are not an island, but here to give inspiration to all. These writings may seem simple...but it is the simplicity of life that makes meaningful marks...

There is so much that has not been said...things that are worthy, but maybe for another time...however I will end these touching moments with something that will always remain tender, deep within my soul...my dear mother would call me dearie so many times *all* my life. To this day I pass that word on to my children to keep that sweet feeling flowing like a soft summer breeze...

In ending this journey with you I want so much to give special importance to growing into people that leave a lasting sweet feeling with all you touch. By so doing it means we have reached the point of loving our fellowman no matter where they are in their walk of life. Yes, that is nearing perfection. In order to be truly happy and content, it is not until we have experienced the joy of seeing someone rejoicing... *because we cared...*

May God bless all my loved ones, my following, and those that have had a very close connection with me through sweet and sad times on my journey to the summit....I am ever so grateful. Blessings to those that knew me little but gave *so much*...It is my sincere prayer that each beating heart will feel the love God has given you and that you will remember what we do for the happiness of others will also nourish our fields of life...

Be still, and know that I am God...Psalms 46:10

Ramona...Fall Concert

My desk where many of my writings took place...

Big Stone Lake...

My Sweet Mother

Fare thee well, my people!
A beautiful tennis day...September 25, 2024...age 95 1/2.

Acknowledgements

Unbelievable...another moment in time I come to you with gratitude for one more book ready for publishing. In my early years the thought of "Author" attached to my name was never a consideration. I was just happy being a quiet little soul walking the earth with a carefree spirit. However, it takes "happenings"...some very strange and unexpected to draw us into the world of writing. So, here I am, one more time...perhaps my last, but praying that all will be sweetly thanked for helping me be where I am today in my journey of travels up the mountain.

I started this book in Florida, then Michigan...a little more in Florida, some in Boston and now in Michigan...it will find its end. Many thoughts were created while walking, sitting at a lakeside, visiting familiar places or the listening to the voice of a young student or tender soul. Most of all inspiration was given from the hearts of many...hidden memories and experiences of those most dear. A little boy, only three years of age left footprints in the sands of my heart...AND all of you that walk or walked my path made your way to my stream of thought. The beautiful music coming from recordings or someone singing or playing the piano...especially one of my family, opened the doors to my memories of special moments in time.

I am so honored to be able to put "thanks"on this page to a very special person in my life...one that patiently, quietly and happily with great enthusiasm stood by me all the way from the beginning to the end of this journey...giving support that no one else could have done so effectively...Cari Haus...may God bless you as you bless others with your beautiful life and wealth of wisdom with many books added to your collection of writings.

My dear friend Eleanore...I could not have completed this book without your love, kindness and graceful support. Thank you! Thank you!

I can't be thankful enough for all the little children up to the teenager that ran to hug me when I appeared at my home on the lake...their beautiful kind loving souls gave me beauty every step of the way in writing my journey. I shall cherish forever their never dying eagerness upon my arrivals...

This book would not be possible without my Heavenly Father, the undying love of my children, grandchildren, loved ones and all that share my path...To you too my dear Buzz, Jai and family in Hawaii. When ending my books, I always think of my dear Diana in Hawaii...all the many weeks and months of stay there because of her very tender love for me. I especially want to thank my sweet daughter-in-law, Jerilyn, for sharing her wonderful family with all of us in such a tender way. They have inspired all of us to a better happy world. With all my heart...I thank each of you...not only for this time in my journey, but for *all* the walks you share and have shared with me. God bless you and all mankind...

www.ingramcontent.com/pod-product-compliance
Lightning Source LLC
Chambersburg PA
CBHW072054150726
47999CB00005B/1782